William B. (William Brisbane) Dick

The American Card-Player

William B. (William Brisbane) Dick

The American Card-Player

ISBN/EAN: 9783741134173

Manufactured in Europe, USA, Canada, Australia, Japa

Cover: Foto ©Lupo / pixelio.de

Manufactured and distributed by brebook publishing software (www.brebook.com)

William B. (William Brisbane) Dick

The American Card-Player

THE
AMERICAN CARD-PLAYER:

CONTAINING

CLEAR AND COMPREHENSIVE DIRECTIONS

FOR PLAYING THE GAMES OF

EUCHRE, WHIST, BÉZIQUE, ALL-FOURS, PITCH, COMMERCIAL PITCH, FRENCH FOURS, ALL FIVES, CASSINO, CRIBBAGE, STRAIGHT AND DRAW POKER, AND WHISKEY POKER:

TOGETHER WITH ALL THE LAWS OF THOSE GAMES.

NEW YORK:
DICK & FITZGERALD, PUBLISHERS.

Entered according to Act of Congress, in the year 1866,

By DICK & FITZGERALD,

In the Clerk's Office of the District Court of the United States for the Southern District of New York.

Lovejoy & Son,
Electrotypers and Stereotypers.
15 Vandewater street N. Y.

CONTENTS.

	PAGE
WHIST	7
Long Whist	8
Short Whist	54
Dumby, or Three-Handed Whist	56
Two-Handed Whist	56
EUCHRE	57
Two-Handed Euchre	79
Three-Handed Euchre	80
Set Back Euchre	81
Lap, Slam, Jambone, and Jamboree	82
CRIBBAGE	85
Five Card Cribbage	86
Six Card Cribbage	101
Three-Handed Cribbage	104
Four-Handed Cribbage	105
BÉZIQUE	112
Bézique without a Trump	119
Bézique Penanche	119
Bézique Limited to a Fixed Point	119
Three-Handed Bézique	120
Four-Handed Bézique	120
ALL-FOURS	121
Four-Handed All Fours	124
Pitch, or Blind All Fours	125
Commercial Pitch, or Auction All Fours	125
All-Fives	127
French Fours	127
CASSINO	128
POKER	130
Straight Poker	130
Draw Poker	132
Whiskey Poker	140
Stud Poker	140
DECISIONS ON DISPUTED POINTS	141
Straight and Draw Poker	141
Euchre	146
All-Fours and Pitch	149
Cassino	151

THE AMERICAN CARD PLAYER.

WHIST.

Of all card games, Whist is perhaps the most interesting; and certainly, if such a term can be used in regard to any thing in which mere chance is an element, the most scientific. As to its absolute origin, it is not necessary for us to inquire whether the game be a simple improvement on the "Ruff and Honors" spoken of by Seymour, or the "Slam," "Whisk," or "Swabbers" with which our forefathers beguiled their evenings in the pre-entertainment ages, which, from the absence of gas, may well be considered dark. Nor is it of much consequence to us whether this particular game of cards was familiar to the Greeks, Romans, Franks, Saxons, or Danes, or whether it was known in England in the days of good Queen Bess. Sufficient for our purpose that it is a good game, and that it has vastly improved since the days when Swift and Congreve played rubbers, and when the game enjoyed the honor of being mentioned in the polished lines of Pope and Thomson. "Whist," says Captain Crawley, "is the king of all card games. Unlike most others, it presents great scope for the exercise of judgment, memory, skill, and good temper. In variety it yields to none, and in scientific calculation it is superior to any. It is not a game determinable by chance alone, for a single error or miscalculation is sufficient to overthrow the apparently most certain triumph. It is an amazing trier of patience, and only he (or she) who can absolutely conquer its difficulties can hope to become a good player. It is necessary to have a 'calculating head' in order to excel, for reflection and memory are the two great qualities at

Whist. Four good players know, almost to a certainty, where every card is placed after the first or second round; and two amateurs against two players stand very little more chance than they would if their cards were laid face upwards on the table." Whist is to be played in silence, for it is not a conversation game. And à propos of the name, here is an anecdote which, whether it be true or not, is worthy of preservation :—The Lords of the three Kingdoms (France, Spain, and Germany), after declaiming all day on affairs of State, found it necessary to rest their tongues at night; so they invented a mute game, and called it *Whist!*

Among the chief writers on Whist since Hoyle, we may mention the names of Deschappelles, Major A. (whose *Short Whist* is a standard authority), Eidrah Trebor (Robert Hardie spelled backwards), J. W. Carleton (the editor of *Bohn's Hand-book of Games*), Mr. Watson, Cœlebs, and Captain Crawley. The gentleman who writes under this *nom de plume* has produced the latest, and perhaps the best work on the game, and to him we are indebted for many valuable hints and maxims.

It must be understood that Hoyle, in all his treatises, presumed that his readers possessed a certain preliminary knowledge of the several games, and that, therefore, a mere reproduction of his *Whist* would be but of small value to amateurs. In the following pages, we assume that our readers have no such previous knowledge, and we therefore begin at the beginning.

THE GAME.

Long Whist is played by four persons, with a *complete* pack of cards, fifty-two in number. The four players divide themselves into two parties, each player sitting opposite his partner. This division is usually accomplished by what is called *cutting the cards*, the two highest and the two lowest being partners; or the partnership may be settled by each player drawing a card from the pack spread out on the table, or in any other way that may be decided on. The holder of the lowest card is the dealer. But previous to their being dealt, the cards are "made"—that is, shuffled—by the elder hand, and "cut" by the younger hand. The undermost card in the pack, after it has been shuffled and cut, is the "trump." These and other terms used in the game we shall presently explain.

The whole pack is now dealt out, card by card, the dealer beginning with the player on his left, the elder hand. The last card—the trump—is then turned face upwards on the table, where it remains till the first trick is won, and turned. The deal completed, each player takes up his allotted thirteen, and arranges them in his hand according to the several suits—the Hearts, Clubs, Spades, and Diamonds by themselves, in their regular order. The elder hand now leads or plays a card. His left-hand adversary follows, then his partner, and last of all his right-hand adversary. Each player must "follow suit," if he can, and the highest card of the suit led wins the "trick;" or if either player cannot follow suit, he either passes the suit—that is, plays some card of another suit—or trumps; that is, plays a card of the same suit or denomination as the turned-up card. Thus, we will suppose the first player leads a Nine of Spades, the second follows with a Ten, the third, who perhaps holds two high cards, plays a Queen, and the last a Two or Three. The trick would then belong to the third player, who won it with his Queen. The winner of the trick then leads off a card, and the others follow as before, and so on till the thirteen tricks are played. A second deal then takes place, as before, and so the game proceeds till one or the other side has obtained ten tricks, which is *game*.

The order and value of the Cards in Whist is as follows:—Ace is highest in play and lowest in cutting. Then follow King, Queen, Knave, Ten, Nine, Eight, Seven, Six, Five, Four, Three, Two, the lowest.

But there are other ways of scoring points besides tricks. The four court cards of the trump suit are called *honors;* and the holders of four, score *four* towards the game; the holders of three, score *two;* but if each player or each set of partners hold *two*, then honors are said to be *divided*, and no points are added to the game on either side. Thus, A. and C. (partners) have between them the Ace, Knave, and Queen. At the end of the deal or round, they say and score *two by honors;* or, B. and D. hold Ace and King only, while A. and C. have Queen and Knave in their hands; then the *honors are divided.*

All tricks above six score to the game. All honors above two score in the way explained—*two* points for *three* honors, *four* points for *four* honors.

There being thirteen tricks which must be made in each round or deal, it follows that seven points may be gained, which, with the four honors, would finish the game in a single deal. This stroke of good fortune is, however, seldom attained. It is much more likely that four or five deals be made before the game is won. As already explained, *ten points* is game in Long Whist.

In Short Whist, which is the ordinary game cut in half, *five points* win. But if either side get up to *nine* points, then the holding of honors is of no advantage. In the language of the Whist-table, *at nine points honors do not count*. But at eight points, the player who holds two honors in his hand has what is called the privilege of *the call*. That is, he may ask his partner if he has an honor—"Can you one?" or "Have you an honor?" If the partner asked does hold the requisite Court card, the honors may be shown, the points scored, and the game ended. But the inquiry must not be made by the player holding the two honors *till it is his turn to play*, nor must the holder of a single honor inquire of his partner if he has two.

Nor does the holding of four honors entitle the partners to show them at any stage of the game except at eight points. To put the matter epigrammatically, *at six or seven points, tricks count before honors; at eight points, honors count before tricks.*

At nine points honors do not count. It must be understood, however, that in order to count honors *at eight points, they must be shown before the first trick is turned, or they cannot be claimed* till the round is completed. Thus it might happen that the partners at eight points, holding the honors between them, and neglecting to show them, would be beaten, even though the other side wanted three or four tricks for the game.

A Single Game is won by the side which first obtains the ten points by a majority of one, two, three, or four points.

A Double Game is made when one side obtains *ten* points before the other has scored *five*.

A Lurch or Triplet is won by the obtainment of ten points to nothing on the other side.

A Rubber is two games won out of three.

The Points of a Rubber are reckoned thus wise:—For the single game, *one* point; for the double, *two* points; and for the rub, *two* points. Thus it is possible to obtain *six* points in one rubber—namely, two doubles and the rub.

The above explanations refer, of course, to games that are played for money stakes, but the more usual plan now a-days is to play

Whist for a small stake on each game, without regard to what are called the *points of the game.*

A *Lurch or Triplet* is in some companies reckoned for *three* points. Generally, however, a lurch is only counted as a double game where triplets are counted; it is possible, therefore, for the winners to obtain *eight* points.

A *Slam* is when the whole thirteen tricks are won in a single hand. It is ordinarily reckoned equal to a full rubber of six points. All these matters are, of course, subject to the practice of, or previous agreement among, the players. If nothing be stated at the commencement of the play, then it would be understood that the stakes played for were determined by each single game.

The game is usually marked on the table by coins or counters, or by the holes in a Cribbage-board. Many pretty little contrivances have been invented as Whist-markers; but if coins be used, the following is the simplest way of arranging them in order to denote the *score*:

```
1     2     3      4      5      6       7       8      9
                                                              o
                          oo     o      ooo     o o     o
                   o                                          o
o    oo    ooo                                                
                   o o    o      ooo     o      o o     o
```

Or thus—a plan in which the unit *above* stands for *three*, or *below* for *five*:

```
4      5       6      7      8       9             9
       o       o                                   o
                     oo     ooo     oooo    or    o
oooo   oo     ooo                                  o
                     o      o       o              
```

But we have not yet quite got over the alphabet of the game. It is absolutely necessary that the   o should make himself fully acquainted with the following—

TECHNICAL TERMS USED IN WHIST.

Ace.—Highest in play, lowest in cutting.
Blue Peter.—A signal for trumps, allowable in modern play. This term is used when a high card is *unnecessarily played* in place of

one of lower denomination, as a ten for a seven, a five for a deuce, &c.

Bumper.—Two games won in succession before adversaries have won one; that is, a rubber of full points—Five at Long Whist, Eight at Short.

Cut.—Lifting the cards when the uppermost portion (not fewer than three) is placed below the rest. The pack is then ready for the dealer.

Cutting-in.—Deciding the deal by each player taking up not fewer than three cards, and the two highest and two lowest become partners. In case of ties, the cards must be cut again.

Cutting-out.—In case of other person or persons wishing to play, the cut is adopted as before, when the highest (or lowest, as may be agreed on) stands out of the game, and does not play.

Call, the.—The privilege of the player at eight points asking his partner if he holds an honor—"Have you one?" The partners having eight points are said to *have the call.* When each side stands at eight, the first player has the privilege. As explained in a previous page, no player can call till it is his turn to play.

Deal.—The proper distribution of the cards, from left to right, face downwards.

Deal, miss.—A misdeal is made by giving a card too many or too few to either player; in which case the deal passes to the next hand. (*See* Laws.)

Deal, fresh.—A fresh or new deal, rendered necessary by any violation of the laws, or by any accident to the cards or players.

Double.—Ten points scored at Long Whist before adversaries have obtained five; or in Short Whist five before three.

Elder-hand.—The player to the left of the dealer.

Faced Card.—A card improperly shown in process of dealing. It is in the power of adversaries in such cases to demand a new deal.

Finessing.—A term used when a player endeavors to conceal his strength, as when, having the best and third best (as Ace and Queen), he plays the latter, and risks his adversary holding the second best (the King). If he succeed in winning with his Queen, he gains a clear trick, because if his adversary throws away on the Queen, the Ace is certain of making a trick. The term finessing may be literally explained by saying a player chances an inferior card to win a trick with while he holds the King card in his hand.

Forcing.—This term is employed when the player obliges his adversary or partner to play his trump or pass the trick. As, for instance, when the player holds the last two cards in a suit, and plays one of them.

Hand.—The thirteen cards dealt to each player.

Honors.—Ace, King, Queen, and Knave of trumps, reckoned in the order here given.

Jack.—The Knave of any suit.

King Card.—The highest unplayed card in any suit; the leading or winning card.

Lead, the.—The first player's card, or the card next played by the winner of the last trick.

Long Trumps.—The last trump card in hand, one or more, when the rest are all played. It is important to retain a trump in an otherwise weak hand.

Loose Card.—A card of no value, which may be thrown away on any trick won by your partner or adversary.

Longs.—Long Whist, as opposed to short.

Lurch.—The players who make the double point are said to have lurched their adversaries.

Love.—No points to score. Nothing.

Marking the Game.—Making the score apparent, with coins, &c., as before explained.

No Game.—A game at which the players make no score.

Opposition.—Side against side.

Points.—The score obtained by tricks and honors. The wagering or winning periods of the game.

Quarte.—Four cards in sequence.

Quarte Major.—A sequence of Ace, King, Queen, and Knave.

Quint.—Five successive cards in a suit; a sequence of five, as King, Queen, Knave, Ten and Nine.

Renounce.—Possessing no card of the suit led, and playing another which is not a trump.

Revoke.—Playing a card different from the suit led, though the player can follow suit. The penalty for the error, whether made purposely or by accident, is the forfeiture of three tricks. (*See* Laws.)

Rubber.—The best two of three games.

Ruffing.—Another term for trumping a suit other than trumps.

Sequence.—Cards following in their natural order, as Ace, King, Queen; Two, Three, Four, &c. There may, therefore, be a sequence of Four, Five, Six, and so on.

Single.—Scoring, at long whist, ten tricks before your adversaries have scored five.

See-saw.—When each partner trumps a suit. For instance, A. holds no Diamonds, and B. no Hearts. When A. plays Hearts, B. trumps and returns a Diamond, which A. trumps and returns a Heart, and so on.

Score.—The points gained in a game or rubber.

Slam.—Winning every trick in a round.

Shorts.—Short whist as opposed to long.

Tenace.—Holding the best and third best of any suit led when last player. Holding tenace; as King and Ten of Clubs. When your adversary leads that suit, you win two tricks perforce. [*Tenace minor* means the second and fourth best of any suit.]

Treble.—Scoring five (at Short Whist) before your adversaries have marked one.

Terce.—A sequence of three cards in any suit.

Terce Major.—Ace, King, and Queen of any suit held in one hand.

Tricks.—The four cards played, including the lead.

Trump.—The last card in the deal; the turn-up.

Trumps.—Cards of the same suit as the turn-up.

Ties.—Cards of like denomination, as two Kings, Queens, &c. Cards of the same number of pips.

Trumping Suit.—Playing a trump to any other suit led.

Underplay.—Playing to mislead your adversaries; as by leading a small card though you hold the King card of the suit.

Younger Hand.—The player to the right of the dealer.

The following are given in most of the treatises on Whist as standing rules for young players. They are of course liable to variation according to the exigencies of the game, as will be seen on perusal of the succeeding pages. Mr. Carleton quotes them without alteration from Watson, who probably got them from some one else. They are known as

BOB SHORT'S RULES

BOB SHORT'S RULES.

FOR FIRST HAND OR LEAD.

1. Lead from your strong suit, and be cautious how you change suits; and keep a commanding card to bring it in again.
2. Lead through the strong suit and up to the weak, but not in trumps, unless very strong in them.
3. Lead the highest of a sequence; but if you have a quart or quint to a King, lead the lowest.
4. Lead through an honor, particularly if the game be much against you.
5. Lead your best trump, if the adversaries be eight, and you have no honor; but not if you have four trumps, unless you have a sequence.
6. Lead a trump if you have four or five, or a strong hand; but not if weak.
7. Having Ace, King, and two or three small cards, lead Ace and King, if weak in trumps, but a small one if strong in them.
8. If you have the last trump, with some winning cards, and one losing card only, lead the losing card.
9. Return your partner's lead, not the adversaries'; and if you have only three originally, play the best; but you need not return it immediately, when you win with the King, Queen, or Knave, and have only small ones, or when you hold a good sequence, have a strong suit, or have five trumps.
10. Do not lead from Ace Queen, or Ace Knave.
11. Do not lead an Ace, unless you have a King.
12. Do not lead a thirteenth card, unless trumps be out.
13. Do not trump a thirteenth card, unless you be last player, or want the lead.
14. Keep a small card to return your partner's lead.
15. Be cautious in trumping a card when strong in trumps, particularly if you have a strong suit.
16. Having only a few small trumps, make them when you can.
17. If your partner refuses to trump a suit, of which he knows you have not the best, lead your best trump.
18. When you hold all the remaining trumps play one, and then try to put the lead in your partner's hand.

19. Remember how many of each suit are out, and what is the best card left in each hand.

20. Never force your partner if you are weak in trumps, unless you have a renounce, or want the odd trick.

21. When playing for the odd trick, be cautious of trumping out, especially if your partner be likely to trump a suit; make all the tricks you can early, and avoid finessing.

22. If you take a trick, and have a sequence, win with the lowest.

FOR SECOND HAND.

23. With King, Queen, and small cards, play a small one, when not strong in trumps. But if weak, play the King. With Ace, King, Queen, or Knave, only, and a small card, play the small one.

FOR THIRD HAND.

24. With Ace and Queen, play her majesty, and if she wins, return the Ace. In all other cases the third hand should play his best card when his partner has led a low one. It is a safe rule for third hand to play his highest.

FOR ALL THE PLAYERS.

25. Fail not, when in your power, to make the odd trick.
26. Attend to the game, and play accordingly.
27. Hold the turn-up card as long as possible, and so keep your adversaries from a knowledge of your strength.
28. Retain a high trump as long as you can.
29. When in doubt win the trick.
30. PLAY THE GAME FAIRLY AND KEEP YOUR TEMPER.

THE LAWS OF WHIST.

Now, it must never be forgotten that in no important particular has the game of Whist been altered since the days of Hoyle. What modern editors have done, has been to render plain the instructions of that excellent authority, and to give in few words what he gave in many.

Well, then, having got so far—having conquered the alphabet of

LAWS AND REGULATIONS. 17

Whist--we come now to consider the laws by which, in all companies, the game is governed. We shall endeavor to make very plain and easy what is necessary to be remembered by all players, giving the laws *pure et simple*, and adding such explanatory remarks as may seem needful in separate paragraphs within brackets.

LAWS OF THE GAME OF WHIST.

CUTTING IN.

1. The two highest are partners against the two lowest.

[Except, of course, in such cases as may be agreed to the contrary. The cutting-in may be done by each player taking a few cards from the pack, and when all have chosen, placing them face upwards on the table. Where the cards are thrown out, and one drawn by each player, this is not necessary.]

2. Less than three cards is not a cut.

[If fewer than three cards be cut off the pack, the player so cutting must replace the cards, and cut again.]

3. In cutting, the lowest card deals, and the Ace is lowest.

[This holds good in most all card games.]

4. Ties must cut again.

[In some companies it is common for *all* players to cut again. In the Clubs, and among regular players, it is sufficient if the two holders of like cards (the tie) take a fresh cut, the highest and the lowest in the second cut becoming partners with the highest and the lowest in the first.]

5. After the pack is cut, no fresh cards can be called for in that deal.

[This is, of course, a Club rule, as is also the following:—"The cards may be changed as often as any player chooses to pay for them."]

6. If a card be exposed, a new cut may be demanded.

[It is important, before the pack be played with, to see that it is perfect, and that it contains no faced cards.]

7. All cutting-in and cutting-out must be by pairs.

[According to the old-established custom, six persons form a full table, and after the first rubber is over, two players retire. Cutting-out determines who shall go out of the game. The two highest retire. Of course the new table cut again for partners.]

8. The right-hand adversary cuts to the dealer.

SHUFFLING.

9 The cards must be shuffled above the table.

[This is absolute in order to prevent any sleight-of-hand in shuffling *below* or *on* the table. By the latter plan, which used to be very common, the position of certain cards might be shown.]

10. Each player has a right to shuffle the cards, the dealer last.

[In practice, the following is the plan most usually pursued:—The left-hand adversary shuffles, or "makes" the cards, and the right-hand adversary cuts them, the dealer's partner not interfering with them at all. It would be well, perhaps, if this plan were regularly followed in all companies.]

DEALING.

11. The cards must be dealt one at a time, commencing with the player to the left of the dealer.

12. In case of a *misdeal*, the deal passes to the next player.

[The following are *misdeals*:—A card too many or too few given to either player. An exposed card. Looking to the trump card before it is turned up in the regular order of play. Dealing the cards with the pack not having been cut. The trump card dropped out of turn. A faulty pack. In every case, except the last, the deal is lost if a fresh deal be claimed by opponents. A card faced by any other than the dealer is not subject to penalty.]

13. The dealer must not touch the cards after they have left his hand, but he is allowed to count those remaining undealt if he suspects he has made a misdeal.

[He may, if he thinks he has made a misdeal, ask his partner and his opponents to count their cards, but it is in their option to comply or refuse. No misdeal can be claimed that is caused by interference of adversaries.]

14. The trump card must be left on the table, face upwards, till the first trick is turned.

[If it is not then taken up, however, it can be treated as an exposed card, and called at any part of the game, provided that no revoke be made by playing it.]

15. One partner may not deal for another without the consent of opponents.

[When ladies play, it is, however, quite usual for their gentlemen partners to deal for them.]

THE GAME.

16. Any card played out of turn can be treated as an exposed card, and called, provided no revoke be thereby caused.

[Thus, a player who wins a trick plays another card before his partner plays to the trick. The second card becomes an exposed card.]

17. If the third player throws down his card before the second, the fourth player has a right also to play before the second: or, if the fourth hand play before the second or third, the cards s

played must stand, and the second be compelled to win the trick if he can.

18. No player but he who made the last trick has a right to look at it after it has been turned.

[This is important, as it is a common error to suppose that the winner of the trick has a right to see the last *three tricks*. Eight cards are all that can ever be seen—that is, the last and the current trick.]

19. A trump card played in error may be recalled before the trick is turned.

[But if the playing of such trump cause the next player to expose a card, such last exposed card cannot be called.]

20. If two cards be played, or if the player play twice to the same trick, his opponents can elect which of the two shall remain and belong to the trick. Provided, however, that no revoke be caused.

[But if the trick should happen to be turned with five cards in it, adversaries may claim a fresh deal.]

21. A player, before he throws, may require his partner to "draw his card," or he may have each card in the trick claimed by the players before the trick is completed.

[The proper way is to say, "Draw your cards," as then the chance of partner claiming the wrong one is lessened.]

22. If two players answer the lead together, the one whose turn it was to play can call the other card in the next or following trick as an exposed card.

23. No player is allowed to transfer his hand to another without the consent of his adversaries.

24. A hand once abandoned and laid down on the table, cannot be taken up again and played.

[It is not sufficient, however, for a player to say, I resign—he must resign absolutely. Cœlebs gives the following in illustration of this law:—"A., having intimated that he has game, B., his adversary, resigns, when it turns out that A. was mistaken. Can B. recall his hand? *Decision*—B. should have called A.'s hand instead of resigning his own. C. and D. proceed to call both hands respectively. A., B. and C. having thrown up their cards, can D. call all *three* hands? *Decision*—His partner's hand can be called by the opponents. A. and B. having thrown up their hand, are respectively permitted to retrieve them; but, after an interval of some tricks, A.'s partner claims to call B.'s hand. Condonation is pleaded, and plea allowed."]

25. If a player announce that he can win every trick, adversaries may call his cards.

THE REVOKE.

26. The penalty for a revoke is the forfeiture of three tricks. If a revoke be made, the adverse party may add three to their score by taking them from their opponents, or they may reduce your score by three.

[In order to more fully explain the intent of a revoke, we quote the following from Mr. Carleton:—"If a suit is led, and any one of the players, having a card of the same suit, shall play another suit to it—that constitutes a revoke. But if the error be discovered before the trick is quitted, or before the party having so played a wrong suit, or his partner, shall play again, the penalty only amounts to the cards being treated as exposed, and being liable to be called."]

27. If a player revokes, and before the trick is turned discovers his error, adversaries may call on him to play his highest or lowest card of the suit led, or they may call the card exposed at any time when such call will not lead to another revoke.

28. No revoke can be claimed till the trick is turned and quitted, or the revoker's partner has played again.

[There are two criteria for the establishment of a revoke, either the trick must have been quitted, or the person revoking, or his partner, must have played since."—*Cœlebs.*]

29. When a revoke is claimed, the cards must not be mixed, under forfeiture of the game.

30. The player or partners against whom a revoke is established cannot claim the game in that deal.

[Thus, if after taking three tricks for the revoke, the offending players should have points enough to make up the ten required for the game, they must remain at nine.]

31. No revoke can be claimed after the cards are out for the next game.

32. When a revoke has occurred on both sides, there must be a new deal.

33. The proof of a revoke is with the claimants, who may examine each trick on the completion of the round.

["There may," says Cœlebs, "be judgment in electing the penalty; *e. g.*, if the opponents are four or two to love, add to your own score; if they are three to one, take them down; if they have seven tricks, take three of them. Bets on the odd trick are decided, in case of a revoke, by the result after the penalty has been exacted."]

CALLING HONORS.

34. Honors cannot be counted unless they are claimed before the next deal. No omission to score them can be rectified after the cards are packed, but an overscore can be deducted.

35. Honors can only be called at eight points, and then only by the player whose turn it is to play.

[If a player calls at eight after he has played, or if any player calls except at the point of eight, it is in the option of the adverse party to call for a new deal. If the trump card is turned, no player must remind his partner to call, under penalty of one point.]

36. At nine points honors do not count.

37. Four honors in one or both partners' hands count *four* to the game; three honors *two*. Two honors on each side are not scored, but are said to be *divided*.

THE SCORE.

38. If both partners score, and a discrepancy occur between them, adversaries may elect which score to retain.

39. The score cannot be amended after the game is won, and the cards packed.

[The manner of keeping the score with counters, &c., is shown at page 11.]

INTIMATIONS BETWEEN PARTNERS.

40. A player may ask his partner, "What are trumps?" or, "Can you follow suit?" "Is there not a revoke?" Or he may tell him to draw his card. All other intimations are unfair.

[The Blue Peter, Tenace, King-card, and various styles of play, cannot be provided for, and are therefore left unmentioned in the laws.]

41. Lookers-on must not interfere unless appealed to.

BY-LAWS.

These are all the *laws* of the game of Whist; but there are certain other rules or by-laws with which it is important the finished player should be acquainted. The penalties attached to a disregard of any of the following by-laws differ in different companies, and to some, which partake rather of the nature of maxims, there is no penalty at all.

When the trump is turned, and taken into the player's hand, it cannot be demanded by either of the players.

When a card is taken distinctly from the hand to which it belongs, it may be treated as an exposed card.

Taking a trick belonging to your adversaries subjects you to no penalty, but it may be reclaimed at any time during the round.

If a player throws up his hand, and the next player follows his example, the game must be considered at an end, and lost to the first player resigning.

Honors scored improperly are in some companies transferred to adversaries.

Approval or disapproval of a partner's play, or, in fact, any improprieties of speech or gesture, are not allowable.

As soon as the lead is played to it is complete.

If a player announce that he can win all the remaining tricks, he may be required to face all his cards on the table. His partner's hand may also be so treated, and each card may be called separately.

HINTS AND CAUTIONS FOR AMATEURS.

Place each suit together, in the natural order of the cards; but do not always put the trumps to the left, as thereby your adversary is able to count them as you put them aside. Many good players do not sort their cards at all, but arrange them in the hand just as they fall on the table.

Never dispute the score, unless you are pretty certain you are right; nothing is so ungraceful as a disputatious player.

Never hesitate long in playing; but if you have a bad hand, do your best and trust to your partner.

Remember that no points can be marked if you neglect to score before the second trick of the succeeding round is played.

Do not show honors after a trick is turned, as they may be called by your adversaries.

At eight points the elder hand asks the younger, and not the younger the elder. That is to say, the player with the two honors in hand asks, "Can you one?"

Remember the good old maxim, "Second hand throws away, and third hand plays high."

Always endeavor to retain a leading card or trump to nearly the end.

Never throw a high card on a lost trick when a low one will suffice.

Follow your partner's lead, and not your adversary's.

When you suspect your partner to be strong in trumps, ruff when he leads a small card and return a little trump.

When your partner leads from an apparently good hand, do your best to assist him.

Whist is a silent game; therefore do not distract the attention of the players by idle conversation.

Never interfere needlessly.

Watch the style of your adversaries' play, and act in accordance with your own judgment.

Make tricks when you can without injury to your partner's hand.

Accustom yourself to remember the cards that are played. A good memory is a wonderful assistant at Whist.

TENACE AND FINESSE.

For the benefit of some beginners, it may be necessary to give a minute definition of two words, which, though universally used, are not generally understood. We mean Tenace and Finesse. Indeed, the game depends so much on the comprehension of their principles, that any man desirous of obtaining even a competent knowledge of it will never regret the trouble of the study. Many parts of Whist are mechanical, and neither maxims nor instructions are necessary to inform the beginner that an Ace wins a King, or that you must follow the suit played, if you have one in your hand.

The principle of the Tenace is simple. If A. has the Ace and Queen of a suit, and B., his adversary, has the King and Knave, the least consideration will show that if A. leads, B. wins a trick, and *vice versa;* of course, in every situation it is the mutual plan of players, by leading a losing card to put it into the adversary's hand, to oblige him to lead that suit, whereby you preserve the Tenace. So far is easily comprehended; but it requires attention with practice to apply the principle, so obvious in the superior to the inferior cards, or see that the same Tenace operates occasionally with the seven and five, as the Ace and Queen, and is productive of the same advantage. A., last player, remains with the Ace and Queen of a suit not played, the last trump and a losing card. B., his left-hand adversary, leads a forcing card. *Query.*—How is A. to play? *Answer.*—If three tricks win the game, or any particular point, he is not to ruff, but throw away his losing card; because his left-hand adversary being then obliged to lead to his suit, he remains Tenace, and must make his Ace and Queen. But, upon the supposition that making the four tricks regains him the rubber, he should then take the force, as in these situations you are justified in giving up the Tenace for an equal chance of making any material point.

The Finesse has a near affinity to the Tenace, except that the latter is equally the object where two, and the former only where there are four, players. A. has the Ace and Queen of a suit led by his partner; now the dullest beginner will see it proper to put on the Queen, and this is called finessing it, and the intention is obviously to prevent the King from making, if in the hand of his right-hand adversary. Should it not be there, it is evident you neither gain nor lose by making the Finesse; but few players carry this idea down to the inferior cards, or see that a trick might be made by a judicious Finesse, against an eight, as a King; but to know exactly when this should be done, requires more skill than in the more obvious cases, united with memory and observation. Another case of Finesse, even against two cards, frequently occurs, and the reason, on reflection, is self-evident. A. leads the ten of a suit of which his partner has the Ace, Knave, and a small one; B. should Finesse or let the ten pass, even though he knows the King or Queen is in his left-hand adversary's hand; because he preserves the Tenace, and probably makes two tricks; whereas, had he put on his Ace, he could make but one—in short, Tenace is the game of position, and Finesse the art of placing yourself in the most advantageous one.

HOW TO PLAY THE GAME SCIENTIFICALLY.

Nothing is so destructive to success in a player as rashness, while, on the other hand, there is nothing to be gained by hesitation. The middle course is the safest.

And now, before we analyze each hand, and show how it should be played, we may profit by an attentive study of Mr. Hoyle's Maxims, as given in the following

GENERAL RULES.

Be cautious how you change suits, and allow no artifice of your adversaries to induce you to do so, without your own hand warrants it.

Keep a commanding card to bring in your own strong suit when trumps are out, if your hand will permit.

Never keep back your partner's suit in trumps, but return them at the first opportunity.

With a strong suit and but few trumps, rather force your adversaries than lead trumps—unless it happens that you are strong in at least one other suit.

Never neglect to make the odd trick when you have a chance.

Look well to your own and your opponents' score, and shape your play by reference to them.

In a backward game, it is sometimes wise to risk one trick in order to secure two; but in a forward game, be more cautious.

If you hold three cards of the suit led by your partner, return his lead with your best.

Remember what cards drop from each hand, how many of each suit are out, and the best remaining card in each.

Seldom lead from Ace and Queen, Ace and Knave, or King and Knave, if you hold another moderate suit.

If neither of your adversaries will lead from the above suits, you must do it yourself with a small card.

You are strong in trumps with five small ones, or three small ones and one honor.

Do not trump a card when you are strong in trumps, more especially if you hold any other strong suit.

If you hold only a few small trumps, make them when you can.

If your partner refuses to trump a suit of which he knows you have not the best, lead him your best trump as soon as you can.

If your partner has trumped a suit, and refuses to play trumps, lead him that suit again.

Never force your partner but when you are strong in trumps, unless you have a renounce yourself, or want only the odd trick.

If the adversaries trump out, and your partner has a renounce, give him that suit when you get the lead, if you think he has a small trump left.

Lead not from an Ace suit originally, if you hold four in number of another suit.

When trumps are either returned by your partner or led by your adversaries, you may finesse deeply in them, keeping the command as long as you can in your own hand.

If you lead the King of any suit, and make it, you must not thence conclude that your partner holds the Ace.

It is sometimes proper to lead a thirteenth card, in order to force the adversary, and give your partner a chance of making a trick as last player.

If weak in trumps, make your tricks soon; but when strong in them, you may play a more backward game.

With five small trumps and a good hand, lead trumps, and so exhaust the suit.

With the lead, and three small trumps and the Ace, it is sometimes judicious to allow your adversaries to make two tricks in trumps with King and Queen, and on the third round play your Ace. You then secure the last trick with your little trump.

With one strong suit, a moderate one, and a single card, it is good play to lead out one round from your strong suit, and then play your single card.

Keep a small card of your partner's first lead, if possible, in order to return it when the trumps are out.

Never force your adversary with your best card of a suit, unless you have the second best also.

In your partner's lead, endeavor to keep the command in his hand, rather than in your own.

If you have a see-saw, it is generally better to pursue it than to trump out, although you should be strong in trumps with a good suit.

Keep the trump you turn up, as long as you properly can.

When you hold all the remaining trumps, play out of them, to inform your partner, and then put the lead into his hand.

It is better to lead from Ace and Nine than from Ace and Ten.

It is better to lead trumps through an Ace or King than through a Queen or Knave.

If you hold the last trump, some winning cards, and one losing card only, lead the losing card.

When only your partner has trumps remaining, and leads a suit of which you hold none, if you have a good sequence of four, throw away the highest of it.

If you have an Ace, with one small card of any suit, and several winning cards in other suits, rather throw away some winning card than that small one.

If you hold only one honor with a small trump, and wish the trumps out, lead the honor first.

If trumps have been led thrice, and there be two remaining in your adversaries' hands, endeavor to force them out.

Never play the best card of your adversaries' lead at second hand, unless your partner has none of that suit.

If you have four trumps, and the command of a suit whereof your partner has none, lead a small card, in order that he may trump it.

With these general directions we may now proceed to consider each hand as analyzed by Hoyle and improved by modern players. The following are from the last and best edition of Hoyle; the maxims have been adopted by Payne, Trebor, Carleton, Cœlebs, Captain Crawley, Matthews, and all the writers on the game.

THE LEAD.

FIRST HAND.

Begin with the suit of which you have the greatest number; for when trumps are out, you will probably make tricks in it.

If you hold equal numbers in different suits, begin with the strongest; it is the least liable to injure your partner.

Sequences are always eligible leads; they support your partner's hand without injuring your own.

Lead from King or Queen, rather than from a single Ace; for since your opponents will lead from contrary suits, your Ace will be powerful against them.

Lead from King rather than Queen, and from Queen rather than Knave; for the stronger the suit, the less is your partner endangered.

Do not lead from Ace Queen, or Ace Knave, till you are obliged; for if that suit be led by your opponents, you have a good chance of making two tricks in it.

In sequences to a Queen, Knave, or Ten, begin with the highest, and so distress your left-hand adversary.

With Ace, King, and Knave, lead the King; if strong in trumps, you may wait the return of this suit, and finesse the Knave.

With Ace, Queen, and one small card, lead the small one; **by** this lead, your partner has a chance of making the Knave.

With Ace, King, and two or three small cards, play Ace and King if weak, but a small card if strong in trumps; when strong in trumps, you may give your partner the chance of making the first trick.

With King, Queen, and one small card, play the small one; for your partner has an equal chance to win, and there is little fear of your making King or Queen.

With King, Queen, and two or three small cards, lead a small card if strong, and the King if weak in trumps; strength in trumps entitles you to play a backward game, and give your partner a chance of winning the first trick. But if weak in trumps, lead the King and Queen, to secure a trick in that suit.

With Ace, with four small cards, and no other good suit, play a small one if strong in trumps, and the Ace if weak; strength in trumps may enable you to make one or two of the small cards, although your partner cannot support your lead.

With King, Knave, and Ten, lead the Ten; if your partner has the Ace, you may probably make three tricks, whether he pass the Ten or not.

With King, Queen, and Ten, lead the King; for if it fail, by putting on the Ten, upon the return of the suit from your partner, you may make two tricks.

With Queen, Knave, and Nine, lead the Queen; upon the return of that suit from your partner, by putting on the Nine, you may make the Knave.

SECOND HAND.

With Ace, King, and small ones, play a small card if strong in trumps, but the King if weak. Otherwise your Ace or King might be trumped in the latter case. Except in critical cases, no hazard should be run with few trumps.

With Ace, Queen, and small cards, play a small one; upon the return of that suit you may make two tricks.

With Ace, Knave, and small cards, play a small one; upon the return of that suit you may make two tricks.

With Ten or Nine, with small cards, play a small one. By this plan, you may make two tricks in the suit.

With King, Queen, Ten, and small cards, play the Queen. By playing the Ten on the return of the suit, you stand a good chance of making two tricks.

With King, Queen, and small cards, play a small card if strong in trumps, but the Queen if weak in them; for strength in trumps warrants a backward game. It is advantageous to keep back your adversaries' suit.

With a sequence to your highest card in the suit, play the lowest of it, for by this means your partner is informed of your strength.

With Queen, Knave, and small ones, play the Knave, because you will probably secure a trick.

With Queen, Ten, and small ones, play a small one, for your partner has an equal chance to win.

With either Ace, King, Queen, or Knave, with small cards, play a small one; your partner has an equal chance to win the trick.

With either Ace, King, Queen, or Knave, with one small card only, play the small one, for otherwise your adversary will finesse upon you.

If a Queen of trumps be led, and you hold the King, put that on; if your partner hold the Ace, you do no harm; and if the King be taken, the adversaries have played two honors to one.

If a Knave of trumps be led, and you hold the Queen, put it on; for, at the worst, you bring down two honors for one.

If a King be led, and you hold Ace, Knave, and small ones, play the Ace, which can only make one trick.

THIRD HAND.

The third hand plays high.

With Ace and King, play the Ace and immediately return the King. It is not necessary that you should keep the command of your partner's hand.

With Ace and Queen, play the Ace and return the Queen. By this means you make a certain trick, though it is sometimes policy to play the Queen. Your partner is, however, best supported by the old-fashioned method.

With Ace and Knave, play the Ace and return the Knave, in order to strengthen your partner's hand.

With King and Knave, play the King; and if it win, return the Knave.

Play the best when your partner leads a small card, as it best supports him.

If you hold Ace and one small card only, and your partner lead the King, put on the Ace, and return the small one; for, otherwise, your Ace may be an obstruction to his suit.

If you hold King and only one small card, and your partner lead the Ace, when the trumps be out play the King; for, by putting on the King, there will be no obstruction to the suit.

FOURTH HAND.

If a King be led, and you hold Ace, Knave, and a small card, play the small one; for, supposing the Queen to follow, you will probably make both Ace and Knave.

When the third hand is weak in his partner's lead, you may often return that suit to great advantage; but this rule must not be applied to trumps, unless you are very strong indeed.

Never neglect to secure the trick if there is any doubt about the game.

If you hold the thirteenth trump, retain it to make a trick when your partner fails in his lead.

If you stand in the nine holes, make all the tricks you can; but at the same time be careful. Watch the game narrowly, and look well to your partner's lead.

LEADING TRUMPS.

Lead trumps from a strong hand, but never from a weak one; by which means you will secure your good cards from being trumped.

Never trump out with a bad hand, although you hold five small trumps; for, since your cards are bad, you only bring out your adversaries' good ones.

If you hold Ace, King, Knave, and three small trumps, play Ace and King; for the probability of the Queen falling is in your favor.

If you hold Ace, King, Knave, and one or two small trumps, play the King, and wait the return from your partner to put on the Knave. By this plan you may win the Queen. But if you have particular reasons to exhaust trumps, play two rounds, and then your strong suit.

If you hold Ace, King, and two or three small trumps, lead a small one, with a view to let your partner win the first trick; but if you have good reason for getting out trumps, play three rounds, or play Ace and King, and then your strong suit.

If your adversaries are eight, and you hold no honor, throw off your best trump; for if your partner has not two honors you lose the game. But if he should happen to hold two honors—as he probably would—you have a strong commanding game.

Holding Ace, Queen, Knave, and small trumps, play the Knave; by this means, the King only can make against you.

Holding Ace, Queen, Ten, and one or two small trumps, lead a small one; this will give your partner a chance to win the first trick, and keep the command in your own hand.

Holding King, Queen, Ten, and small trumps, lead the King; for if the King be lost, upon the return of trumps you may finesse the Ten.

Holding King, Knave, Ten, and small ones, lead the Knave; it will prevent the adversaries from making a small trump.

Holding Queen, Knave, Nine, and small trumps, lead the Queen; if your partner hold the Ace, you have a chance of making the whole suit.

Holding Queen, Knave, and two or three small trumps, lead the Queen.

Holding Knave, Ten, Eight, and small trumps, lead the Knave; on the return of trumps you may finesse the Eight.

Holding Knave, Ten, and three small trumps, lead the Knave; this will most distress your adversaries, unless two honors are held on your right hand, the odds against which are about three to one.

Holding only small trumps, play the highest; by which means you support your partner.

Holding a sequence, begin with the highest; thus your partner is instructed how to play his hand, and cannot be injured.

If any honor be turned up on your left, and the game much against you, lead a trump as soon as you can. You may thus probably retrieve an almost lost game.

In all other cases it is dangerous to lead through an honor without you are strong in trumps, or have an otherwise good hand. All the advantage of leading through an honor lies in your partner finessing.

If the Queen be turned up on your right, and you hold Ace, King, and small ones, lead the King. Upon the return of trumps finesse, unless the Queen falls. Otherwise the Queen will make a trick.

With the Knave turned up on your right, and you hold King, Queen, and Ten, the best play is to lead the Queen. Upon the return of trumps play the Ten. By this style of play you make the Ten.

If the Knave turns up on your right, and you hold King, Queen, and small ones, it is best to lead the King. If that comes home, you can play a small one, for the chance of your partner possessing the Ace.

If Knave turn up on your right, and you have King, Queen, and Ten, with two small cards, lead a small one. Upon the return of trumps play the Ten. The chances are in favor of your partner holding an honor, and thus you make a trick.

If an honor be turned up on your left, and you hold only one honor with a small trump, play out the honor and then the small one. This will greatly strengthen your partner's hand, and cannot injure your own.

If an honor be turned up on the left, and you hold a sequence, lead the highest; it will prevent the last hand from injuring your partner.

If a Queen be turned up on the left, and you hold Ace, King, and a small one, lead the small trump; you have a chance for winning the Queen.

If a Queen be turned up on your left, and you hold Knave with small ones, lead the Knave; for the Knave can be of no service, since the Queen is on your left.

If an honor be turned up by your partner, and you are strong in trumps, lead a small one; but if weak in them, lead the best you have. By this means the weakest hand supports the strongest.

If an Ace be turned up on the right, and you hold King, Queen, and Knave, lead the Knave: it is a secure lead.

If an Ace be turned up on the right, and you hold King, Queen, and Ten, lead the King; and upon the return of trumps play the Ten. By this means you show strength to your partner, and probably make two tricks.

If a King be turned up on the right, and you hold Queen, Knave, and Nine, lead the Knave, and upon the return of trumps, play the Nine; it may prevent the Ten from making.

If a King be turned up on your right, and you hold Knave, Ten, and Nine, lead the Nine; upon the return of trumps play the Ten. This will disclose your strength in trumps to your partner.

If a Queen be turned up on the right, and you have Ace, King, and Knave, lead the King. Upon the return of trumps play the Knave, which makes a certain trick.

HOW TO PLAY WHEN YOU TURN UP AN HONOR.

If you turn up an Ace, and hold only one small trump with it, if either adversary lead the King, put on the Ace.

But if you turn up an Ace, and hold two or three small trumps with it, and either adversary lead the King, put on a small one; for if you play the Ace, you give up the command in trumps.

If you turn up a King, and hold only one small trump with it, and your right-hand adversary lead a trump, play a small one.

If you turn up a King, and hold two or three small trumps with it, if your right-hand adversary lead a trump, play a small one.

If you turn up a Queen or Knave, and hold, besides, only small trumps, if your right-hand adversary lead a trump, put on a small one.

If you hold a sequence to the honor turned up, play it last.

HOW TO PLAY FOR THE ODD TRICK.

Never trump out if you can avoid it, for you can hardly be sure of the other three hands.

If your partner, by hoisting the Blue Peter, or by any other allowable intimation, shows that he has means of trumping any suit, be cautious how you trump out. Force your partner, if strong in trumps, and so make all the tricks you can.

Make tricks early in the game, and be cautious in finessing.

With a single card of any suit, and only two or three small trumps, lead the single card.

RETURNING PARTNER'S LEAD.

In the following cases it is best to return your partner's lead directly:

When you win with the Ace, and can return an honor; for then it will greatly strengthen his hand.

When he leads a trump; in which case return the best remaining in your hand, unless you hold four. An exception to this arises if the lead is through an honor.

When your partner has trumped out; for then it is evident he wants to make his strong suit.

When you have no good card in any other suit; for then you are entirely dependent on your partner.

In the following instances it is proper that you should NOT *return your partner's lead immediately:*

When you win with the King, Queen, or Knave, and have only small cards remaining. The return of a small card will more distress than strengthen your partner's hand.

When you hold a good sequence; for then you may make tricks, and not injure his hand.

When you have a strong suit. Leading from a strong suit is a direction to your partner, and cannot injure him.

When you have a good hand; for in this case you have a right to consult your own hand, and not your partner's.

When you hold five trumps; for then you are warranted to play trumps if you think it right.

When, in fine, you can insure two or three tricks, play them, and then return the lead. With a leading hand it is well to play your own game.

THE FINISH.

The most important part of a game at Whist is the Finish—the last two or three tricks. Be careful how you play, or you may make a bad ending to a good beginning.

Loose Cards.—If you hold three winning cards and a loose one, play the latter, and trust to your partner.

Loose Trump and Tenace.—Holding these, play the loose trump.

King and the Lead.—If you hold a King and a loose card, the best plan is to play the last, so that your partner may lead up to your King.

Long Trumps.—If you hold three, it is best to lead the smallest; by this means you give your partner a chance of making tricks, and still hold a commanding card in your own hand. It is not well to play out the King card.

Third Hand with King, &c.—"Supposing," says Cœlebs, "ten tricks being made, you remain with King, Ten, and another. If second hand plays an honor, cover it; otherwise finesse the Ten for a certain trick. It you want two tricks play your King."

Running a Card.—The same authority says—"With such cards as Knave, Nine, Eight against Ten guarded, by 'running' the Eight you make every trick."

CASES IN POINT.

The following cases are given by Hoyle:

I.

If A. and C. are partners against B. and D., and eight trumps have been played out, and A. has four trumps remaining, B. having the best trump and is to lead, should B. play his trumps or not? No; because as he would leave three trumps in A.'s hand, if A.'s partner has any capital suit to make, by B.'s keeping the trump in his hand he can prevent his making that suit.

II.

A. and C. are partners against B. and D.; twelve trumps are played out, and seven cards only remain in each hand, of which A. has the last trump, and likewise the Ace, King, and four small cards of a suit; question, whether A. should play the Ace and King of that suit or a small one? A. should play a small card of that suit, as it is an equal bet his partner has a better card in that suit than the last player, and, in this case, if four cards of the suit happen to be in either of the adversaries' hands, by this manner of playing he will be enabled to make five tricks in that suit. Should neither of the adversaries have more than three cards in that suit, it is an equal bet that he wins six tricks in it.

III.

Supposing three hands of cards, containing three cards in each hand, let A. name the trumps, and let B. choose which hand he pleases—A. having the choice of either the other two hands, will win two tricks. Clubs are trumps: first hand, Ace, King, and Six of Hearts; second hand, Queen and Ten of Hearts, with Ten of Trumps; third hand, Nine of Hearts, with Two and Three of Trumps. The first hand wins of the second, the second wins of the third, and the third wins of the first.

IV.

THE ADVANTAGE BY A SEE-SAW.

Suppose A. and B. partners, and that A. has a quart-major in Clubs, they being trumps, another quart-major in Hearts, another quart-major in Diamonds, and the Ace of Spades; and let us suppose the adversaries, C. and D., to have the following cards, viz., C. has four Trumps, eight Hearts, and one Spade; D. has five Trumps and eight Diamonds: C. being to lead, plays a Heart, D. trumps it; D. plays a Diamond, C. trumps it; and thus pursuing the saw, each partner trumps a quart-major of A.'s, and C. being to play at the ninth trick, plays a Spade, which D. trumps: Thus C. and D. have won the first nine tricks, and leave A. with his quart-major in Trumps only.

The foregoing case shows, that whenever you gain the advantage of establishing a saw, it is your interest to embrace it.

STRENGTH IN TRUMPS.

The following hands are given by Hoyle to demonstrate what is known as being strong in trumps:—

Ace, King, and three small trumps.
King, Queen, and three small trumps.
Queen, Ten, and three small trumps.
Queen and four small trumps.
Knave and four small trumps.
Five trumps without an honor must win two tricks if led.

FORCING YOUR PARTNER.

You are justified in forcing your partner if you hold—
Ace and three small trumps.
King and three small trumps.
Queen and three small trumps.
Knave and four small trumps.
Five trumps.

CASE TO DEMONSTRATE THE DANGER OF FORCING YOUR PARTNER.

Suppose A. and B. partners, and that A. has a quint-major in trumps, with a quint-major and three small cards of another suit, and that A. has the lead; and let us suppose the adversaries, C. and D., to have only five trumps in either hand; in this case, A. having the lead, wins every trick.

INDICATIONS AND INFERENCES.

The following are given by Mr. Carleton as allowable indications between partners, or hints from your adversaries' play :—

Should the Ace fall from the second hand in the first round of a suit, it is fair to conclude that he is either very strong in it, or has only the one card.

Should there be a renounce in which a court card is thrown away, it indicates that the holder of it has a high sequence in the suit, or perhaps no other, or wishes a trump played.

When you have played all your trumps, avoid playing a suit from which your partner threw away, when he could no longer follow your trump lead. He is weak in that suit. If he has thrown away more than one suit, play that from which he threw away last.

When a suit is ruffed, and he who wins plays the Ace of trumps and then stops, be sure that is the last of his trumps.

Should you hold the next best of a sequence that has been led, you may suspect the lead was from a single card, and with a view to a ruff.

When there is no call at the point of eight, and you do not hold an honor yourself, the chances are your partner has two. You may model your game by that presumption.

With Ace, King, win with the King; if leader, begin with the King; and if it be trumped, or you think right to change the suit, your partner will guess where the Ace is.

The call at eight is a hint to your partner to play trumps.

When the last player wins with a high card, and then leads a lower one of the same suit, with which he might equally have taken the trick, it is assumed that he has the intermediate cards.

Leading a small card for your partner's Ace shows that you have the King.

To these may be added the Blue Peter, as described in a former page.

HOYLE'S GRAMMAR OF WHIST.

How should sequences of trumps be played?—Begin with the highest.

When sequences are not in trumps, how should they be played?—If you hold five, begin with the lowest; if less than five, begin with the highest.

Why are sequences preferable to frequent changes of suits?—Because they form safe leads, and gain the tenace in other suits.

When should partners make tricks early?—When they are weak in trumps.

When may you allow your opponents to make tricks early in the round?—When you are strong in trumps.

When is it proper to play from an Ace-suit?—When you hold three Aces, neither of which is a trump.

When any good card is turned up on your right, how should you play?—If an Ace be turned up, and you hold King and a small card, play the small one. If King be turned up, and you hold Ace and small ones, play a small one. If a Ten be turned up, and you hold King, Knave, Nine, and others, begin with the Knave, in order to prevent the Ten from making a trick, and then finesse with the Nine.

How do you know when your partner has no more of the suit played?—By his playing his high card instead of a loose one. Thus, suppose you hold King, Queen, and Ten, and your partner answers with Knave, you may be certain that is the only card he possesses of the suit.

When ought you to over-trump your adversary, and when not?—If you are strong in trumps, you may throw away a loose trump; but if weak, over-trump at all risks.

If your right-hand adversary lead a suit in which you have Ace, King, and Queen, with which card are you to take the trick?—With the Queen, as then the same suit may be led again by your opponent, under the idea that his partner holds the high cards.

Why should you play from King-suit rather than from Queen-suit, though you may possess a like number of each?—Because, it is two to one that the Ace does not lie in your adversary's hands, and it is five to four that if you play from Queen you lose her.

When you possess the four best cards of any suit, why do you play your best?—To inform your partner as to the state of your hand.

The Queen turned up on your right, and you hold Ace, Ten, and one trump; or King, Ten, and one trump, if right-hand opponent plays the Knave, what should you do?—Pass the trick. You cannot lose by so doing, as your Ace must make, and you may gain a trick.

When can you finesse in other suits with impunity?—When you are strong in trumps.

EXAMPLES FROM HOYLE.

In order to fully conquer the difficulties of Whist and achieve success, it is necessary, indeed, to *persevere to the end*. "Never despair" is an excellent motto for a whist-player. Having carried the student safely over the *pons asinorum*, let us now take a leaf or two direct from Hoyle. Hitherto it has been our endeavor to improve upon the instructions of our great authority by carefully comparing his maxims with those of later writers, and embodying with them the results of modern card-table experience. In this chapter we shall give the *ipsissima verba* of Edmond Hoyle from the last and best of the authorized editions of his treatise on Whist, believing that a careful perusal of the following examples cannot but prove of considerable use to all who would become thoroughly familiar with the game.

PARTICULAR GAMES, AND THE MANNER IN WHICH THEY ARE TO BE PLAYED AFTER A LEARNER HAS MADE SOME PROGRESS IN THE GAME.

I.

"Suppose you are elder hand, and that your game consists of King, Queen, and Knave of one suit; Ace, King, Queen, and two small cards of another suit; King and Queen of the third suit, and three small trumps; *Query*, how is this hand to be played? You are to begin with the Ace of your best suit (or a trump), which informs your partner that you have the command of that suit; but you are not to proceed with the King of the same suit, but you must play a trump next; and if you find your partner has no strength to support you in trumps, and that your adversary plays to your weak suit—

viz., the King and Queen only—in that case play the King of the suit which belongs to the best suit; and if you observe a probability of either of your adversaries being likely to trump that suit, proceed then and play the King of the suit of which you have the King, Queen and Knave. If it should so happen that your adversaries do not play to your weakest suit, in that case, though apparently your partner can give you no assistance in trumps, pursue your scheme of trumping out as often as the lead comes into your hand; by which means, supposing your partner to have but two trumps, and that your adversaries have four each, by three rounds of trumps, there remain only two trumps against you."

II.

ELDER HAND.

"Suppose you have Ace, King, Queen, and one small trump, with a sequence from the King of five in another suit, with four other cards of no value. Begin with the Queen of trumps, and pursue the lead with the Ace, which demonstrates to your partner that you have the King, and as it would be bad play to pursue trumps the third round till you have first gained the command of your great suit, by stopping thus. it likewise informs your partner that you have the King and one trump only remaining; because if you had Ace, King, Queen, and two trumps more, and trumps went round twice, you could receive no damage by playing the King the third round. When you lead sequence. begin with the lowest; because, if your partner has the Ace. he plays it, which makes room for your suit. And since you have let your partner into the state of your game, as soon as he has the lead, if he has a trump or two remaining, he will play trumps to you with a moral certainty that your King clears your adversaries' hands of all their trumps."

III.

SECOND PLAYER.

"Suppose you have Ace, King, and two small trumps, with a quint-major of another suit, in the third suit you have three small cards, and in the fourth suit one. Your adversary on your right hand begins with playing the Ace of your weak suit, and then proceeds to play the King. In that case do not trump it, but throw away a losing card, and if he proceeds to play the Queen, throw away another losing card, and do the like the fourth time, in hopes your partner may trump it, who will in that case play a trump, or will play to your strong suit. If trumps are played, go on with them two rounds, and then proceed to play your strong suit; by which means, if there happens to be four trumps in one of your adversary's hands, and two in the other, which is nearly the case, your partner being entitled to have three trumps out of the nine, consequently there remain only six trumps between the adversaries; your strong suit forces their best trumps, and you have a probability of making the odd trick in your own hand only; whereas, if you had trumped one of your adversaries' best cards, you had so weakened your hand as probably not to make more than five tricks without your partner's help."

IV.

"Suppose you have Ace, Queen, and three small trumps, Ace, Queen, Ten, and Nine of another suit, with two small cards of each of the other suits; your partner leads to your Ace, Queen, Ten and Nine; and as this game requires rather to deceive adversaries than to inform your partner, put up the Nine, which naturally leads the adversary to play trumps, if he wins that card. As soon as trumps are played to you, return them upon your adversary, keeping the command in your own hand. If your adversary who led trumps to you puts up a trump which your partner cannot win, if he has no good suit of his own to play, he will return your partner's lead, imagining that suit lies between his partner and yours. If this finesse of yours should succeed, you will be a great gainer by it, but scarcely possible to be a loser."

PARTICULAR GAMES BOTH TO ENDEAVOR TO DECEIVE AND DISTRESS YOUR ADVERSARIES, AND TO DEMONSTRATE YOUR GAME TO YOUR PARTNER.

I.

"Suppose I play the Ace of a suit of which I have Ace, King, and three small ones; the last player does not choose to trump it, having none of the suit; if I am not strong enough in trumps I must not play out the King, but keep the command of that suit in my hand by playing of a small one, which I must do in order to weaken his game."

II.

"If a suit is led, of which I have none, and a moral certainty that my partner has not the best of that suit, in order to deceive the adversary I throw away my strong suit; but to clear up doubts to my partner when he has the lead I throw away my weak suit. This method of play will generally succeed, unless you play with very good players, and even with them you will oftener gain than lose by this method of play."

PARTICULAR GAMES TO BE PLAYED, BY WHICH YOU RUN THE RISK OF LOSING ONE TRICK ONLY TO GAIN THREE.

I.

"Suppose Clubs to be trumps, a Heart is played by your adversary; your partner having none of that suit, throws away a Spade; you are then to judge his hand is composed of trumps and Diamonds; and suppose you win that trick, and being too weak in trumps, you dare not force him; and suppose you shall have King, Knave, and one small Diamond; and further, suppose your partner to have Queen and Five Diamonds; in that case, by throwing out your King in your first lead, and your Knave in your second, your partner and you may win five tricks in that suit; whereas, if you had led a small Diamond, and your partner's Queen having been won with the Ace, the King and Knave remaining in your hand, obstructs his suit; and though he may have the long trump, yet, by playing a small Diamond, and his long trump having been forced out of his hand, you lose by this method of play three tricks in that deal."

II.

"Suppose in the like case of the former, you should have Queen, Ten, and one small card in your partner's strong suit; which is to be discovered by the former example; and suppose your partner to have Knave and five small cards in his strong suit; you having the lead are to play your Queen, and when you play again you are to play your Ten; and suppose him to have the long trump, by this method he makes four tricks in that suit; but should you play a small one in that suit, his Knave being gone, and the Queen remaining in your hand in the second round of playing that suit, and the long trump being forced out of his hand, the Queen remaining in your hand obstructs the suit, by which method of play you lose three tricks in that deal."

III.

" In the former examples you have been supposed to have had the lead, and by that means have had an opportunity of throwing out the best cards in your hand of your partner's strong suit, in order to make room for the whole suit; we will now suppose your partner is to lead, and in the course of play it appears to you that your partner has one great suit; suppose Ace, King, and four small ones, and that you have Queen, Ten, Nine, and a very small one of that suit; when your partner plays the Ace, you are to play the Nine; when he plays the King, you are to play the Ten; by which means you see, in the third round, you make your Queen, and having a small one remaining, you do not obstruct your partner's great suit; whereas, if you had kept your Queen and Ten, and the Knave have fallen from the adversaries, you would have lost two tricks in that deal."

IV.

" Suppose in the course of play, as in the former case, you find your partner to have one great suit, and that you have King, Ten, and a small one of that suit; your partner leads the Ace, in that case play your Ten, and in the second your King; this method is to prevent a possibility of obstructing your partner's great suit."

V.

" Suppose your partner has Ace, King, and four small cards in his great suit, and that you have Queen, Ten, and a small card in that suit; when he plays his Ace, do you play your Ten, and when he plays his King, do you play your Queen; by which method of play you only risk one trick to get four."

SOME DIRECTIONS FOR PUTTING UP AT SECOND HAND KING, QUEEN, KNAVE, OR TEN OF ANY SUIT, ETC.

I.

"Suppose you have the King and one small card of any suit, and that your right-hand adversary plays that suit; if he is a good player do not put up the King, unless you want the lead, because a good player seldom leads from a suit of which he has the Ace, but keeps it in his hand (after the trumps are played out) to bring in his strong suit."

II.

"Suppose you have a Queen and one small card of any suit, and that your right-hand adversary leads that suit, do not put on your Queen, because, suppose the adversary has led from the Ace and Knave, in that case, upon the return of that suit, your adversary finesses the Knave, which is generally good play, especially if his partner has played the King; you thereby make your Queen; but by putting on the Queen, it shows your adversary that you have no strength in that suit, and consequently puts him upon finessing upon your partner throughout that whole suit."

III

"In the former examples you have been informed, when it is thought proper to put up the King or Queen at second hand; you are likewise to observe, in case you have the Knave or Ten of any suit, with a small card of the same suit, it is generally bad play to put up either of them at second hand, because it is five to two that the third hand has either Ace, King, or Queen of the suit led; it therefore follows, that as the odds against you are five to two, and though you should succeed sometimes by this method of play, yet in the main you must be a loser, because it demonstrates to your adversaries that you are weak in that suit, and consequently they finesse upon your partner throughout that whole suit."

IV.

"Suppose you have Ace, King, and three small cards of a suit; your right-hand adversary leads that suit; upon which you play your Ace, and your partner plays the Knave. In case you are strong in trumps, you are to return a small one in that suit, in order to let your partner trump it. And this consequence attends such play, viz., you keep the command of that suit in your own hand, and at the same time it gives your partner an intimation that you are strong in trumps; and therefore he may play his game accordingly, either in attempting to establish a saw, or by trumping out to you, if he has either strength in trumps or the command of the other suits."

SOME DIRECTIONS HOW TO PLAY WHEN AN ACE, KING, OR QUEEN ARE TURNED UP ON YOUR RIGHT HAND, ETC.

I.

"Suppose the Ace is turned up on your right hand, and that you have the Ten and Nine of trumps only, with Ace, King, and Queen of another suit, and eight cards of no value, *quere*, how must this game be played? Begin with the Ace of the suit of which you have the Ace, King, and Queen, which is an information to your partner that you have the command of that suit; then play your Ten of trumps, because it is five to two that your partner has King, Queen, or Knave of trumps; and though it is about seven to two that your partner has not two honors, yet, should he chance to have them, and they prove to be the King and Knave, in that case, as your partner will pass your Ten of trumps, and as it is thirteen to twelve against the last player for holding the Queen of trumps, upon supposition your partner has it not, in that case, when your partner has the lead, he plays to your strong suit, and upon your having the lead, you are to play the Nine of trumps, which puts it in your partner's power to be almost certain of winning the Queen if he lies behind it.

"The foregoing case shows, that turning up of an Ace against you may be made less beneficial to your adversaries, provided you play by this rule."

II.

"If the King or Queen are turned up on your right hand, the like method of play may be made use of; but you are always to distinguish the difference of your partner's capacity, because a good player will make a proper use of such play, but a bad one seldom, if ever."

III.

"Suppose the adversary on your right hand leads the King of trumps, and that you should have the Ace and four small trumps, with a good suit; in this case it is your interest to pass the King; and though he should have King, Queen, and Knave of trumps, with one more, if he is a moderate player, he will play the small one; imagining that his partner has the Ace; when he plays the small one, you are to pass it, because it is an equal wager that your partner has a better trump than the last player; if so, and that he happens to be a tolerable player, he will judge you have a good reason for this method of play, and consequently, if he has a third trump remaining he will play it; if not, he will play his best suit."

THE TEN OR NINE BEING TURNED UP ON YOUR RIGHT HAND, ETC.

I.

"Suppose the Ten is turned up on your right hand, and that you should have King, Knave, Nine, and two small trumps, with eight other cards of no value, and that it is proper for you to lead trumps, in that case begin with the Knave, in order to prevent the Ten from making of a trick; and though it is but about five to four that your partner holds an honor, yet if that should fail, by finessing your Nine on the return of trumps from your partner, you have the Ten in your power."

II.

"The Nine being turned up on your right hand, and that you should have Knave, Ten, Eight, and two small trumps, by leading the Knave it answers the like purpose of the former case."

III.

"You are to make a wide difference between a lead of choice and a forced lead of your partner's; because, in the first case he is supposed to lead from his best suit, and finding you deficient in that suit, and not being strong enough in trumps, and not daring to force you, he then plays his next best suit; by which alternation of play, it is next to a demonstration that he is weak in trumps. But should he persevere, by playing of his first lead, if he is a good player, you are to judge him strong in trumps, and it is a direction for you to play your game accordingly."

IV.

"There is nothing more pernicious at the game of Whist than to change suits often, because in every new suit you run the risk of giving your adversary the tenace; and therefore, though you lead from a suit of which you have the Queen, Ten, and three small ones, and your partner puts up the Nine only, in that case, if you should happen to be weak in trumps, and that you have no tolerable suit to lead from, it is your best play to pursue the lead of that suit by playing your Queen, which leaves it in your partner's option whether he will trump it or not, in case he has no more of that suit; but in your second lead, in case you should happen to have the Queen or Knave of any other suit, with one card only of the same suit, it would be better play to lead from your Queen or Knave of either of these suits, it being five to two that your partner has one honor at least in either of those suits."

V.

"If you have Ace, King, and one small card of any suit, with four trumps; if your right hand adversary leads that suit, pass it, because it is an equal wager that your partner has a better card in that suit than the third hand; if so, you gain a trick by it; if otherwise, as you have four trumps, you need not fear to lose by it, because, when trumps are played, you may be supposed to have the long trump."

CAUTION NOT TO PART WITH THE COMMAND OF YOUR ADVERSARIES' GREAT SUIT, ETC.

I.

"In case you are weak in trumps, and that it does not appear that your partner is very strong in them, be very cautious how you part with the command of your adversaries' great suit. For suppose your adversary plays a suit of which you have King, Queen, and one small card only, the adversary leads the Ace, and upon playing the same suit, you play your Queen, which makes it almost certain to your partner that you have the King; and suppose your partner refuses to that suit, do not play the King, because, if the leader of that suit or his partner have the long trump, you risk the losing of three tricks to get one."

II.

" Suppose your partner has ten cards remaining in his hand, and that it appears to you that they consist of trumps and one suit only; and suppose you should have King, Ten, and one small card of his strong suit, with Queen and two small trumps; in this case, you are to judge he has five cards of each suit, and therefore you ought to play out the King of his strong suit; and if you win that trick, your next play is to throw out the Queen of trumps; if that likewise comes home, proceed to play trumps. This method of play may be made use of at any score of the game, except at 4 and 9."

THE TRUMP TURNED UP TO BE REMEMBERED.

" It is so necessary that the trump turned up should be known and remembered, both by the dealer and his partner, that we think it proper to observe, that the dealer should always so place that card as to be certain of having recourse to it. For suppose it to be only a Five, and that the dealer has two more—viz., the Six and Nine—if his partner trumps out with Ace and King, he ought to play his Six and Nine; because, let us suppose your partner to have Ace, King, and four small trumps, in this case, by your partner's knowing you have the Five remaining, you may win many tricks."

TWO TRUMPS.

The following Case happens frequently :—

" That you have two trumps remaining when your adversaries have only one, and it appears to you that your partner has one great suit; in this case always play a trump, though you have the worst; because, by removing the trump out of your adversaries' hands, there can be no obstruction to your partner's great suit."

FIVE TRUMPS.

" Suppose you have five trumps, and six small cards of any suit, and you are to lead; the best play is to lead from the suit of which you have six, because, as you are deficient in two suits, your adversaries will probably trump out, which is playing your own game for you; whereas, had you begun with playing trumps, they would force you, and consequently destroy your game."

CALCULATIONS FOR BETTING.

Among modern players, heavy betting at cards has nearly gone out. Whist is now generally played for a simple stake—so much per game—so much per rubber; but as no treatise on the game can be considered complete without a table of chances, we give the calculations of Hoyle, as improved by modern practice.

AT LONG WHIST—

It is about five to four that your partner holds one card out of any two.

Five to two that he holds one card out of any three.

Two to one that he does not hold a certain named card.

Three to one that he does not hold two out of three named cards in a suit.

Three to two that he does not hold two cards out of any four named.

Five to one that your partner holds one winning card.

Four to one that he holds two.

Three to one that he holds three.

Three to two that he holds four.

Four to six that he holds five.

BETTING THE ODDS.

The odds on the rubber is five to two in favor of the dealers generally.

With the first game secured, the odds on the rubber, with the deal, are—

1	to love	about	7	to	2
2	—	—	4	—	1
3	—	—	9	—	2
4	—	—	5	—	1
5	—	—	6	—	1

At any part of the game, except at the points of eight and nine, the odds are in proportion to the number of points required to make the ten required. Thus, if A. wants four and B. six of the game, the odds are six to four in favor of A. If A. wants three and B. five, the odds are seven to five on A. winning the game.

At the commencement of the game it is about $\frac{1}{20}$ per cent. in favor of the dealer.

The odds against the dealer counting two for honors (that is, three honors in hand) are about nearly four to one.

Against the dealer and his partner holding the four honors, the odds are at least six to one. Against the non-dealers holding the four honors, the odds are about twenty to one, because it is only fifty-two to sixteen, or a little more than nine to one that an honor is turned up.

Against honors being divided, the odds are about three to two against either side, though the dealers have certainly the best chance.

The following, calculated strictly, are the

ODDS ON THE GAME WITH THE DEAL.

1 love is 11 to 10		4 to 3 is 7 to 6
2 love — 5 — 4		5 — 3 — 7 — 5
3 love — 3 — 2		6 — 3 — 7 — 4
4 love — 7 — 4		7 — 3 — 7 — 3
5 love — 2 — 1		8 — 3 — 7 — 2
6 love — 5 — 2		9 — 3 — 3 — 1
7 love — 7 — 2		
8 love — 5 — 1		5 to 4 is 6 to 5
9 love — 9 — 2		6 — 4 — 6 — 4
		7 — 4 — 2 — 1
1 to 1 is 9 to 8		8 — 4 — 3 — 1
2 — 1 — 9 — 7		9 — 4 — 5 — 2
3 — 1 — 9 — 6		
4 — 1 — 9 — 5		6 to 5 is 5 to 4
5 — 1 — 9 — 4		7 — 5 — 5 — 3
6 — 1 — 3 — 1		8 — 5 — 5 — 2
7 — 1 — 9 — 2		9 — 5 — 2 — 1
8 — 1 — 4 — 1		
		7 to 6 is 4 to 3
3 to 2 is 8 to 7		8 — 6 — 2 — 1
4 — 2 — 4 — 3		9 — 6 — 7 — 4
5 — 2 — 8 — 5		
6 — 2 — 2 — 1		8 to 7 is 3 to 2
7 — 2 — 8 — 3		9 — 7 — 12 — 8
8 — 2 — 4 — 1		
9 — 2 — 7 — 2		

ODDS ON THE GAME. 51

Honors counting at eight points and not at nine, the odds are slightly in favor of the players at eight. It is usual for the players at eight points, with the deal, to bet six to five on the game. It is about an even bet, if honors are not claimed at eight points, that the dealers win. As a disinterested piece of advice, however, let us add—*Don't bet at all.*

AT SHORT WHIST.

The following are the generally accepted odds; but it must be remembered that, in respect of betting, the chances in Short Whist do not greatly differ from those of the old and, as we think, much superior game:—

ON THE GAME WITH THE DEAL.

At starting, the odds are about 11 to 10, or perhaps 21 to 20, in favor of the dealers. With an honor turned up, the odds are nearly a point greater in favor of the dealers.

1 to love is about	10 to 8
2 —	5 — 3
3 —	3 — 1
4 —	4 — 1

2 to 1 is about	5 to 4
3 — 2 —	2 — 1
3 — 3 —	11 — 10
4 — 3 —	9 — 7

ON THE RUBBER WITH THE DEAL.

1 to love is about	7 to 4
2 —	2 — 1
3 —	9 — 2
4 —	5 — 1

The following are given as mere matters of curiosity.

It is 50 to 1 against the dealer holding 7 trumps, neither more nor less.

15 to 1 against his holding 6 trumps.
8 to 1 against his holding exactly five.
3 to 2 against his holding exactly 4.
5 to 2 in favor of his holding 3 or more trumps.
11 to 2 in favor of his holding 2 or more trumps.
30 to 1 against his holding only the one trump turned up.

AGAINST ANY NON-DEALER HOLDING ANY SPECIFIED NUMBER OF TRUMPS.

100 to 1 against his holding exactly 7.
30 to 1 " " 6.
15 to 1 " " 5.
5 to 1 " " 4.
3 to 2 " " 3.
5 to 2 in favor of his holding 2 or more.
50 to 1 in favor of his holding 1 trump or more.

Against the dealer holding 13 trumps, it is calculated to be 158,753,389,899 to 1.

Against his holding 12 trumps, 338,493,367 to 1.

Against his holding 11 trumps, 3,000,000 to 1.

Against his holding 10 trumps, 77,000 to 1.

Against his holding 9 trumps, 3500 to 1.

Against his holding 8 trumps, 320 to 1.

Against his holding 7 trumps, 50 to 1.

These figures are, however, of but small practical utility in Whist from the simple fact that now-a-days such odds are seldom or never offered or taken. Whist is not a game to gamble at.

L'ENVOY.

The reader who has accompanied me thus far will at least acknowledge that there is more in a game at Whist than appears at first sight. In the Clubs it is played scientifically; and with regular players two packs of cards are always brought in, kept on the table, and played with alternately each deal. This saves some trouble and time, as, while the one pack is being gathered by the younger hand, the elder hand "makes" the other. This plan likewise prevents a wide-awake player from "placing" cards in shuffling, and so obtaining a slight advantage by knowing whereabout in the pack certain cards are likely to be.

The reader must not, however, imagine that he is a Whist-player because he has read this or any other treatise on the game. An ounce of practice is worth a pound of theory; and all that books can do is to teach the theory and principles of the game. Any lady or gentleman can become a good player with a little care and attention. The good player will read the rules and maxims with attention, and profit by them; but only the real lover and master of the game will be able to tell when he may depart from both with safety. There is all the difference in the world between slavishly following written instructions and adapting them to particular circumstances. As in life, so in Whist—you must use your own educated judgment if you would succeed. Practice makes perfect; and there is no royal road to Whist any more than there is to learning.

My readers will allow me, I am sure, to warn them that Whist is an amusement, not a labor; and that it is best played at the table. The amateur should never play a card without a reason for it; a bad reason is better than playing at random without any reason at all. Coolness, memory, and good temper are the three great secrets of success at Whist. Play the game well, and be cautious how you finesse. Take care of your trumps, and do not throw them away unnecessarily. It is good play, if you hold four leading cards in a suit, to exhaust that suit before you play another; as then, when trumps are out, you make a trick by leading the thirteenth card. It is judicious to force the strong hand, bad to force the weak one. Never throw away a trick without good reason, and avoid ruffing your right-hand adversary's lead, if you can without danger. Establish your long suit, if possible; and do not over-trump your right-hand opponent without you see absolute necessity. The first object is to win the game, the second to save it; therefore, nothing venture nothing have. Always return your partner's lead in trumps; having regard, however, always to your own hand. Endeavor to retain the turn-up and a commanding card as long as you can. Inform your partner of your strength in trumps by the allowable intimations —such as throwing a best card to a partner's winning card, playing the highest of a sequence when fourth player, and so on. Try to stop a long suit of your adversaries by playing a trump, without fear of being over-trumped. Look carefully at your hand to avoid making a revoke; and watch your opponents' play, in order to detect one. It is quite fair to deceive your adversaries by underplay, and the use of the Blue Peter is acknowledged in all companies, though it was quite unknown to Hoyle. Endeavor to thoroughly comprehend the principle of tenace, as this is a most valuable adjunct at Whist. Look well after the score, and play out your long suit as soon as you can. The playing of a single card is generally successful, as, if it makes a trick, you can then trump when your partner returns the lead, and perhaps establish a see-saw.

Patient study and long practice are as necessary to make a good Whist-player as to make a good mathematician. But courtesy and willingness to acknowledge and forgive errors are no small recommendations: therefore, to lady and gentleman players I may say *Omnibus Placeto.*

SHORT WHIST, DUMBY, DOUBLE DUMBY, &c

SHORT WHIST.

It is scarcely necessary to expend much time in describing Short Whist, its principles being precisely the same as those of the older and now almost universal game. The game about which Hoyle wrote was Whist, which was, some years ago, cut in half, in order to suit the taste of some aristocratic players. The story goes that the operation was performed by Lord Peterborough, at Bath, in order that he might the more quickly recover some heavy losses, or make them still heavier. After enjoying considerable popularity for nearly half a century, Short Whist is now on the decline. The real differences between the two games are very slight, and perhaps it may be sufficient for the reader if I give merely

THE LAWS OF SHORT WHIST.

1. The game consists of five points. One point scored saves the triple game; three points, a double. The rubber is reckoned at two points.

[Eight points may therefore be gained in a single rubber.]

2. Honors cannot be "called" at any part of the game, and do not count at the point of four.

[In all other respects, honors are reckoned as in Long Whist.]

3. The two highest and two lowest are partners, the lowest cut having the deal.

[The cards are to be shuffled and cut in precisely the same way as in the old-fashioned game.]

4. An exposed card necessitates a fresh deal.

5. In cases of misdeal, the deal passes to the next player.

[Misdeals occur from precisely the same causes as in Long Whist, and need not, therefore, be stated.]

6. No questions as to either hand can be asked after the trick is turned.

[Nor are any questions except those admissible in the other game to be asked.]

7. Any card played out of turn, or shown accidentally, can be called.

8. A revoke is subject to the penalty of three tricks.

[Taken as in Long Whist.]

9. The side making the revoke remains at four, in whatever way the penalty be enforced.

10. Lookers-on must not interfere, unless appealed to by the majority of the players.

It is not necessary to dilate upon the best method of playing each separate hand at this game, because whatever is useful and true at Long Whist is equally useful and true at Short Whist. "The peculiarities of the short game," says a recent writer, "call for special appliances. This should act as stimulants to the player, and rouse his energy." But what these special appliances are it is difficult to discover, seeing that the two games are identical in every thing but length. The only advantage of the short game lies in the more forcible use that can be made of trumps. "Trumps," says Carleton, "should be your rifle-company; use them liberally in your manœuvres; have copious reference to them in finessing, to enable you to maintain a long suit. Should you be weak in trumps, ruff a doubtful card at all times; with a command in them, be very chary of that policy. Let your great principle always be to keep the control of your adversaries' suit, and leave that of your partner free. If you see the probable good effect of forcing, decide which of your adversaries you will assail, but do not attempt them both at once. Let it be the stronger if possible. When you force both hands opposed to you, one throws away his useless cards; while the chance is, the other makes trumps that, under other circumstances, would have been sacrificed." And so, *et cetera ad infinitum.* Deschapelles, who is the French Hoyle without his science, but with double his power of writing, says of Short Whist:—"When we consider the social feelings it engenders, the pleasure and vivacity it promotes, and the advantages it offers to the less skilful player, we cannot help acknowledging that Short Whist is a decided improvement upon the old game." All this is, however, open to argument; and therefore *de gustibus non est.*

DUMBY, OR THREE-HANDED WHIST.

This game is precisely the same as Long Whist, only that one player takes two hands, one of which he holds in the usual manner, and the other he spreads open on the table. The rules are the same.

Another Game is played by three persons, in which two Nines and Fours, and one of the Fives is cast out from the pack, and each player plays on his own account.

A third way of playing Three-handed Whist is to reject the fourth hand altogether, and allow it to remain unseen on the table. Each player then takes the miss, or unseen hand, in exchange for his own, if he thinks fit. Each player stands on his cards, and the best hand must win. There is, however, room for finesse, and the player who sees two hands—the miss, and that first dealt to him—has an undeniable advantage.

TWO-HANDED WHIST.

This game is either played as Double Dumby, by exposing two hands and playing as with four players, or by rejecting two hands, and each player making the best he can of his own hand. In these games each honor counts as one point in the game. There is but small room for skill in any of the imperfect Whist-games, and the player who is acquainted with the real old-fashioned game need not be told how to play his cards at Dumby or French Humbug. At best, these games are inferior to Cribbage, Ecarté, All-Fours, or any of the regular two-handed games.

EUCHRE.

THE origin of this fascinating game is somewhat uncertain. From the fact that the word *Bauer*, a peasant, is pronounced similarly to the names of the two leading cards in the game, some have supposed it to be of German invention. Yet the game is unknown in Germany, except in those parts where it has been introduced by wandering Americans. Others assumed that it had a nautical origin, and was invented by some old salt—the names given the commanding cards having reference to the forward anchors of the ship. As it has been traced to the counties of Lancaster, Berks, and Lehigh, in Pennsylvania, where it first made its appearance about forty years since, it is not difficult to conjecture how it arose. Some rich German farmer's daughter, of these Americo-Teutonic regions, had been visiting Philadelphia in the winter. While there she had stayed at the house of some relative, whose girls spent their summers among the Lehigh hills; and she carried home a confused memory of Ecarté. On her dim account, some one of her ingenious rural beaux had created the rudiments of the present game, with the name corrupted to Euchre. By additions and alterations it grew to be what it is. Conjectural as this may appear, a number of corroborative facts seem to indicate that it is the truth.

RULES AND TECHNICAL TERMS OF EUCHRE.

ADOPTING.—*Synonyme*—"Taking it up." This is the privilege of the dealer, after the others have passed, to discard an inferior card, and use instead the trump card turned up. The words used are, "I take it up."

ALONE.—Playing without the assistance of your partner, when you have a hand which it is probable would take five tricks. The words are, "I play alone," or "Alone," or "Cards away," or "I try it."

Rule 1.—A player can only play alone when he adopts, orders up, or makes a trump, or when his partner assists, orders up, or makes a trump. He cannot, however, play alone with a trump he has passed, or with a trump, the making of which he has passed.

A player cannot play alone when he or his partner is ordered up by an opponent, or when the opposite side adopts or makes the trump. Only those can play alone who have legally taken the responsibility of the trump, and may be euchred; therefore, when one player legally elects to play alone, neither of his opponents can play alone against him.

Rule 2.—If the elder hand passes, and his partner offers to play it alone, the elder hand cannot come in and play it alone, but must turn his cards face down, and go out.

Rule 3.—When your partner plays alone, you must always lay down your cards, or place them under the pack, without exposing their faces. (See RESPONSIBLE, and Rule 36.)

Rule 4.—A player who goes alone, must announce his intention in a clear and audible way and tone, so that no doubt can be entertained of his design. If he expresses his purpose in a vague and ambiguous manner, so that it is not clearly understood by his adversaries, and he or they make a lead, he forfeits his privilege, and must play with his partner.

ASSIST.—If, when your partner deals, and the eldest hand passes, you know by your hand alone, or by comparing it with the deckhead, that you can make three tricks, you may say to him, "I assist." This is equivalent to ordering up the trump into his hand, for he thereupon discards his poorest card, and the trump card is his to play when he needs it.

BOWER.—The Jack or Knave of the trump suit, and of the suit of the same color.

BRIDGE.—This is where one side has scored four, and the other one or two.

Rule 5.—When your opponents have one or two and you have four, if you are eldest hand, unless you have one trick certainly in your hand—that is, the right bower, or the left bower guarded—you will order it up whether you have a trump or not, to prevent them going alone, and making four tricks.

CALL.—The right to demand an exposed card.*

Rule 6.—If your *right-hand adversary* plays a card out of turn, or shows it, you can require him to lead it when his turn comes, or play it when his turn comes, and that suit is required, or if he would be otherwise privileged to play it, whether it be to his advantage or not.

Rule 7.—A party refusing to play an exposed card on call, forfeits two to his opponents, as in a revoke.

*(See " *Decisions on Disputed Points*," notes *IV.* and *V., Euchre, pages* 148 *and* 149.)

TECHNICAL TERMS.

"CARDS AWAY."—The same as, "I play alone."

COUNT.—To reckon the game.

Rule 8.—An error in count can be rectified at any time before the next deal is completed.

COUNTERS.—The trey and quatre are used in marking game. The face of the trey being up, and the face of the quatre down on it, counts *one*, whether one, two, or three pips are exposed; the face of the quatre being up, and the trey over it, face down, counts *two*, whether one, two, three, or four of the pips are shown; the face of the trey uppermost counts *three*; and the face of the quatre uppermost counts *four*. The deuce and trey are now rarely used as counters, being more liable to mistakes.

COAT-CARDS.—The Bower, King, and Queen, from the fact that they are coated, or dressed.

COURT-CARDS.—The same as coat-cards.

CROSS THE SUIT.—To make a trump of a different color from the card turned up by the dealer.

Rule 9.—If your partner turns down, and the making is passed to you, either pass or cross the suit. The exceptions to this rule are only to be learned by practice.

CUT.—To separate the shuffled pack into two parts, a right possessed by the right-hand opponent.

Rule 10.—A cut must not be less than three cards removed from the top, nor must it be made so as to leave less than four cards at bottom; and the pack must be put on the table for the cut.

DEAL.—To distribute the cards to which each player is entitled. You give each player five cards, in two rounds, commencing with your left-hand opponent. You begin by first dealing two cards to each, and then three.

Rule 11.—Every player cuts for the deal at the outset of the game; the highest getting the deal; and if there be a tie, the parties tied cut again.

Rule 12.—In cutting, the Ace is lowest, and the Jack the highest, the others having their regular numerical order.

Rule 13.—If a party lets a card fall in cutting, that is his cut; and if he shows two, the highest is his cut.

Rule 14.—In dealing, you may begin by giving first two, and then three cards round to each party, or *vice versa*; but you cannot begin by dealing two to one, three to the next, and so on.

Rule 15.—The cards may be shuffled by others than the dealers, but the dealer must always shuffle last. If the dealer makes a misdeal, he forfeits the deal to the eldest hand.

Rule 16.—If a card is turned or faced in dealing, a new deal may be demanded, but the right to deal is not lost.

Rule 17.—If any opponent takes up or looks at his cards before the trump card is turned up, the dealer does not lose his deal, in case of a misdeal.

Rule 18.—If a deal is made out of turn, it is good, provided it be not discovered until the trump card is turned, and one of the parties have looked at their hands.

Rule 19.—If an opponent displays a card dealt, the dealer may make a new deal, unless he or his partner has first examined his own cards.

Rule 20.—If the pack is discovered to be defective, by reason of having more or less than thirty-two cards, the deal is void; but all the points before made are good.

DEALER.—One who distributes the cards.

DECK.—The same as Pack.

DECK-HEAD.—The card turned up as trump.

DISCARD.—Putting a card out of the dealer's hand, face down, under the pack, when he "takes it up" in lieu of the trump card on the deck.

Rule 21.—In discarding, you put away any card not a trump, no matter how valuable, that will give you a chance to trump that suit. For instance, if Hearts be trumps, and your lay cards are the Ace of Spades, and the Queen of Clubs, and Eight of Clubs, discard the Ace of Spades.

Rule 22.—The discard is not complete until the card is under the pack; and if the eldest hand plays before the discard is complete, the dealer may change the card, or may go it alone, though a card has been led.

DUTCH IT.—To make a trump of the color that is turned down.

Rule 23.—When your opponent turns it down, it is your policy to make it the next in suit, that is, to name the trump of the same color, unless you have a commanding hand in one of the cross suits.

ELDEST HAND.—The left-hand adversary of the dealer, so called because he is the first to play.

EUCHRE.—The failure of that side which makes, orders up, or takes up a trump, to take three tricks; this failure scoring two points to their adversaries.

FACE-CARD.—The coat-cards.

FACED CARD.—One with its face turned up in shuffling, cutting, or dealing.

FINESSE.—This is where a player holding the best and third best trump, plays the latter first, taking the risk that his opponents do not hold the second best trump, or that his partner does. In either case he wins the two tricks.

FORCE.—To lead a suit of which your opponents hold none, thus obliging them to trump or lose the trick.

GAME.—When one party makes five points before the other.

GO ALONE.—Synonymous with "play alone."

GUARDED.—Having a strong card of another suit behind your trumps; or having a smaller trump behind a strong one.

HAND.—The five cards dealt to each player.

INFORMATION.—Any thing passing from one partner to another, by which the latter knows how to play.

Rule 24.—If a player indicates his hand by words or gestures to his partner, directs him how to play, even by telling him to follow the rules of the game, or in any way acts unfairly, the adversary scores one point.

Rule 25.—If a player, when they are at a bridge, calls the attention of his partner to the fact, so that the latter orders up, the latter forfeits the right to order up, and either of the opponents may play alone, if they choose so to do.

"What are trumps?" "Draw your card." "Can you not follow suit?" "I think there is a revoke?"

The above remarks, or those analogous, are the only ones allowed to be used, and they only by the person whose turn it is to play.

LAY-CARD.—Any card other than trump.

LAY-SUIT.—Any suit not a trump.

LEAD.—The right to play first. The first card played.

LEFT BOWER.—The Knave of the same color as the trump suit.

LEFT BOWER GUARDED.—The Left Bower protected by another trump.

LONE HAND.—A hand so strong in trumps alone, or in trumps, guarded by high cards of a lay suit, that it will probably win five tricks if its holder plays alone.

LONE PLAYER.—The one playing without his partner.

LOVE-GAME.—Scoring five points to your adversary's none.

MAKING A POINT.—Where the responsible wins the odd trick.

MAKING THE TRUMP.—Naming a new suit for trump, after the dealer has turned the trump card down.

Rule 26.—Any player making a trump cannot change the suit after having once named it; and if he should by error name the suit previously turned down, he forfeits his right to make the trump, and such privilege must pass to the next eldest player.

MARCH.—Where all the tricks are made by one side.

MARKING THE GAME.—Counting.

MISDEAL.—An error in giving out the cards, forfeiting the right to the deal, unless the dealer be interfered with, as elsewhere provided. (See DEAL.)

NEXT IN SUIT.—Dutching it.

NUMERICAL CARDS.—Those neither ace nor face.

ODD TRICK.—The third trick.

ORDERING UP.—Requiring the dealer and his partner to play the trump as it has been turned.

PACK.—The ordinary pack of cards, with the smaller cards from Deuces to Sixes, inclusive, thrown out.

PARTNER.—The one joined with you in playing against your adversary.

Rule 27.—The penalty of the misconduct of one partner falls on both.

PASS.—To decline to play at the trump turned up.

PASS AGAIN.—To decline the privilege of making a new trump, after the first has been turned down.

PIP.—The marks or spots on the inferior cards.

PLAY ALONE.—To play a hand without one's partner.

POINT.—One of the five required for the game.

REVOKE.—Playing a card of a different suit from that demanded This is sometimes vulgarly called renig.

Rule 28.—When a player revokes, the adversaries add two to their score.

Rule 29.—A revoke is not complete until the trick is quitted, and the revoker, or his partner, has played again.

Rule 30.—Though the revoker can correct his error, before he or his partner has played a second time, yet the opponent can call the exposed card if it be the revoker's next lead, or his turn to play one of that suit.

Rule 31.—When the revoker corrects his error, his partner, if he has played, cannot change his card played; but the adversary may, if he could have played another card before.

Rule 32.—When a revoke is claimed against adversaries, if they mix their cards, or throw them up, the revoke is taken for granted, and they lose the two points.

Rule 33.—No party can claim a revoke after cutting for a new deal.

Rule 34.—A revoke on both sides, forfeits to neither; but a new deal must be had.

Rule 35.—If a point has been made by a revoke, it must be taken from the score of the offender.

RANK.—The relative power of the cards, commencing and going down, in trumps, as follows: Right Bower, Left Bower, Ace, King, Queen, Ten, Nine, Eight, Seven; but in the Lay Suits the Jacks take place between the Queens and Tens.

RESPONSIBLE.—The party who order up a trump, assist, make a trump, or take it up.

Rule 36.—None have the privilege of playing alone, except those who take the responsibility of the trump.

RIGHT BOWER.—The Jack of trumps.

RIGHT BOWER FOLLOWED.—The Right Bower with another trump behind.

ROUND.—The four cards in a trick.

RUBBER.—The best two of three games.

RUFFING.—Another term for trumping a suit other than trumps.

SCORE.—The points gained in a game or rubber.

SEQUENCE.—The numerical succession of cards of the same color.

SHUFFLE.—To mix the cards before dealing.

SIDE-CARDS.—Lay cards.

SLAM.—Love-game, vulgarly called "a skunk."

SPOT.—The marks on the inferior cards.

STOCK.—To fraudulently shuffle the cards so as to deal what cards are desired for the dealer. The cards not dealt out.

SUIT.—Each separate set of the four denominations of cards in the pack; as the suit of Hearts, the suit of Diamonds, &c.

TAKING IT UP.—Indorsing the trump by the dealer, and discarding another card for it, after the rest have passed.

Rule 37.—The dealer who takes it up must let the trump remain on the talon until it is necessary to play it on a trick.

TALON.—The cards remaining in the pack after a deal.

TENACE.—Where the last player holds in his hand the highest and third best of the cards out.

THROW AWAY.—To play a worthless card on a trick, when you cannot follow suit, and do not desire to trump; as, for instance, where it is your partner's.

THROWING UP.—Tossing one's cards on the table.

Rule 38.—Throwing up a hand is giving up the points; and if the cards are turned face up, the left-hand player may call them as he thinks proper, and they must be played accordingly.

TRICK.—The same as Round.

Rule 39.—No player has a right to see any trick but the last.

TRUMP.—The suit turned up, or made the commanding suit.

TRUMP CARD.—The card which is turned up by the dealer after the hands have been dealt around.

TURN DOWN.—The trump card which is turned face downward on the talon by the dealer, after all have passed.

TURN UP.—The trump card.

UNDERPLAYING.—Following suit with a low card, when you have one in your hand superior to your adversary's.

EUCHRE, AND HOW TO PLAY IT.

The game of Euchre is played with thirty-two cards, all below the denomination of seven-spot being rejected. Four persons constitute the complement for the game, and partners are determined by dealing and turning up one card to each; those receiving the two lowest cards, and *vice versa*, being associated together.

VALUE OF THE CARDS.

The value of the cards in Euchre is the same as in Whist, All-Fours, and other games, excepting that the Knave of the suit corresponding with the trump is called the *Right Bower*, and is the highest card of the hand; and the other Knave of the same color is called the *Left Bower*, and is the card of second importance. For example: if Hearts should be turned trump, the Knave of Hearts is the highest card, the Knave of Diamonds second in value, and the Ace, King, Queen, &c., of Hearts, then come in their regular order, as at Whist. When the Knaves are of the opposite color from the trump card, they rank no higher than at Whist.

THE DEAL.

The players usually cut for deal, and he who cuts the highest Euchre card is entitled to the deal, and that is accomplished by giving the eldest hand, or first person to the left of the dealer, two cards, and so on all around, and then dealing an additional three cards to each player, in the same order. Regularity should be observed in dealing, and no party should be allowed to receive from the dealer, in any round, more than the number of cards given to the eldest hand. For instance, if the dealer begins by giving the left-hand player two cards, he cannot be allowed to vary, so as to give another three, and then two again, but must continue as he began. The proper manner of dealing is as we pointed out at the outset, and should be rigidly observed.

The advantage which accrues to the dealer is manifest. From the manner in which cards are played in all games, those of a corresponding suit will necessarily fall together, and therefore the dealer enhances his prospects thirty-three and one-third per cent. for an additional trump by dealing three cards last round, for then he has the three immediately preceding the trump, when, if he had began the deal with three cards, he would end by having only the two cards preceding the trump.

After five cards have been dealt to each player, in the order as above, the dealer turns up the top card on the pack or talon, which is called the trump. After the first hand, the deal passes to each player, in rotation.

THE GAME.

The game consists of five points—the parties getting that number first being winners—and the points are indicated by the number of tricks taken by the players. If all the tricks are taken by one side it constitutes what is technically termed a *march*, and entitles the fortunate parties to a count of two; and it is necessary to take three tricks in order to count one, or "make a *point*," as it is called. Taking four tricks counts no more than three.

When the trump is turned, the first person to the left of the dealer looks at his cards, for the purpose of determining what he intends to do, whether to "pass" or "order the trump up;"

and this, to a certain extent, will depend upon the strength of his hand. If he holds cards of sufficient value to secure three tricks, he will say, "I order it up," and the dealer is then obliged to take the card turned up, and discard one from his hand; and the card thus taken up becomes the trump. If the eldest hand has not enough strength to order it up, he will say, "I pass," and then the partner of the dealer has to determine whether he will "pass" or "assist." If he has enough, with the help of the card his partner has turned, to make three tricks, he will say, "I assist," and the card is taken up as before. If he passes, then it goes to the third hand, who proceeds exactly as the eldest hand. Should all the players pass, it becomes the dealer's privilege to announce what he will do, and, if he thinks he can take three tricks, he says, "I take it up," and immediately discards his weakest card, placing it under the remainder of the pack, and, instead of the card thus rejected, he takes that turned up, which remains the trump. It is not considered *en regle* for the dealer to remove the trump card until after the first trick has been taken, unless he needs it to play. It is let lay that every one may see what the trump is. We may as well state here, that it is always the dealer's privilege to discard any one card in his hand, and take up the trump card; and this holds good whether he is assisted by his partner, is ordered up by his adversaries, or takes it up himself. This gives the parties having the deal an advantage about equal to one trick. Should the dealer not be confident of winning three tricks, he says, "I turn it down," and, at the same time, places the turn-up card, face down, on the pack. Should all the players decline to play at the suit turned up, and the dealer turn it down, the eldest hand is then entitled to make trump what he chooses (excepting the suit already turned down). If the eldest hand is not strong enough in any suit, and does not wish to make the trump, he can pass again, and so it will go in rotation, each one having an opportunity to make the trump, in his regular turn, to the dealer. If all the players, including the dealer, decline the making of the trump, the deal is forfeited to the eldest hand. The eldest hand, after the dealer has discarded, opens the game, and leads any card he chooses. The person playing the highest card takes the trick, and he in his turn is obliged to lead. In this manner the game proceeds, until the five cards in each hand are exhausted. Players are required, under penalty of the loss of two points, to follow suit. If, however, they cannot, why then they may throw away a small card, or trump at their pleasure.

The trey and quatre are used in marking game. The face of the trey being up, and the face of the quatre down on it, counts *one*, whether one, two, or three pips are exposed; the face of the quatre being up, and the trey over it, face down, counts *two*, whether one, two, three, or four of the pips are shown; the face of the trey uppermost counts *three;* and the face of the quatre uppermost counts *four*. The deuce and trey are now rarely used as counters, being more liable to mistakes.

It may be laid down as one of the general rules of Euchre, that whatever is undertaken by a player must be accomplished, in order to make the point. For instance, if I adopt, or order up the trump, and fail in securing three tricks, it is called being "Euchred," and entitles the opponents to a count of two; or if I make the trump after the original one has been turned down, and do not secure three tricks, I am also "Euchred," and it counts as before. Therefore it will be perceived, that in order to properly play the game, one should have, in addition to the ordinary rules, a thorough knowledge of the theory of chances, as they apply to this game, and exercise it judiciously.

ADOPTING, OR TAKING UP THE TRUMP.

As to what constitute sufficient force of cards to take the trump up, is a matter of considerable importance to the player. The purpose being to make a point, of course there must be a reasonable probability of securing three tricks, and this probability should be made, to a certain extent, dependent upon the position of the game. If the dealer should be three or four on the score, while the opponents are one or two, the deal might be passed by turning the trump down, and still the chances of gaining the game be not materially reduced; but if the position should be reversed, why then the dealer would be warranted in attempting the hazard upon a light hand, as the prospects of defeat with the deal in his favor would be no greater than the percentage of the same against him. Of course, any player would know that his success would be beyond peradventure, if holding both Bowers and the Ace; but the moment you attempt to point out what any thing less would avail, you depart from the scope of argument, predicated upon substantial bases, to the unsubstantial realms of hypotheses. Any thing less than both Bowers and the Ace *might* be Euchred, and the plodding player who exhausted his time in the search of absolute certainty might be beaten a hundred times by the cards which he had rejected. It is generally accepted as "sound doctrine," that three trumps—two of them being Court Cards, backed by a Lay Ace—is sufficient to attempt a point. The player must note the state of the game, and act accordingly. If the game stand four and four, it is better for you to take up the trump on a small hand than leave it to your adversaries to make. Suppose the game is three and three, you should be very careful of adopting the trump on a weak hand, because a Euchre puts your opponents out.

PASSING AND ORDERING UP.

No prudent player will "order" the trump unless he holds enough to render his chances of success beyond reasonable doubt. There are times and positions of the game when, however, there would be no imprudence in "ordering" up upon a light hand; for instance, supposing the game to stand four and four, the dealer turns the trump, and either the eldest or third hand has an ordinary good show of cards, with nothing better of another suit, there it would be proper to "order up," for, should the trump be turned down, your chances of success would be lost, and in case you are Euchred, it would but give the game to those who would win it anyhow at another suit.

If the position of the player is eldest hand, and a suit should be turned, in which he receives both Bowers and another large trump, and he has also two cards of the corresponding suit in color, it would clearly be his policy to pass, for the obvious reason, that if the dealer's partner should assist, he would be enabled to Euchre the opposing side, and, if the trump were turned down, his hand would be just as good in the next suit; and having the first opportunity of making the trump, he could go it alone, with every probability of making the hand and scoring four.

Should the eldest hand hold the Right Bower, Ace, or King, and another small trump, and a card of the same color as the trump suit, it would be good play to pass; for if your adversaries adopt the trump, you will, in all probability, Euchre them; and if they reject it, you can make the trump next in suit, and the chances of scoring a point are in your favor.

When you are four, and hold commanding trumps sufficient to make a sure point, order up, particularly if you are eldest hand, for then you will take your opponent's deal.

As a general rule the eldest hand should not order up the trump unless he has good commanding cards, say, Right Bower, King and Ten of trumps, with a lay ace of a different color, or Left Bower, King, and two numerical trumps. The player at the right of the dealer should hold a very strong hand to order up the trump, because his partner has evidenced weakness by passing, and if the opposing side turn down the trump, his partner has the first say to make a new trump.

MAKING THE TRUMP.

In case the dealer turns the trump down, the eldest hand has the privilege of making it what he pleases, and the rule to be generally followed is, if possible, to Dutch it, *i. e.*, to make it next in suit, or the same color of the trump turned. The reason for this is very evident. If Diamonds should be the trump turned, and the dealer refuse to take it up, it would be a reasonable supposition that neither of the Bowers were in the hands of your opponents; for if the dealer's partner had held one of them, he would in all probability, have assisted; and the fact of its being turned down by the dealer also, raises the presumption that he had neither of them. Then, in the absence of either Bower, an otherwise weak hand could make the point in the same color. For reverse reasons, the partner of the dealer would cross the suit, and make it Clubs or Spades; as his partner had evidenced weakness in the red suits, by turning a red card down, it would be but fair to presume that his strength was in the black.

Be careful how you make the trump when your adversaries have scored three points, and, as a general rule, do not make or order up a trump unless you are eldest hand.

ASSISTING.

"Assisting" is where your partner is the dealer, and, with the help of the card he has turned trump, you deem your hand sufficient to take three tricks. In other words, suppose the Ace of Hearts to be turned, and you hold the Left Bower and King: you say to your partner, "I assist," and then he is obliged to take up the Ace turned, and discard, the same as though he had taken it up voluntarily. Two Court Cards is considered a good "assisting" hand; but where the game is very close, of course it is advisable to assist, even upon a lighter hand; for if the game stands four and four, the first hand will "order up," if the card turned is the best in his hand, and therefore the fact of his passing would be an evidence of weakness.

When assisted by your partner, and you hold a card next in denomination to the card turned up (whether higher or lower,) play it as opportunity offers. For instance, if you turn up the Ace, and hold either the left Bower or King, when a chance occurs play the Bower or King, and thus inform your partner that you have the Ace remaining. The same policy should be adopted when your partner assists and you have a sequence of three trumps, the trump card being the smallest of the three, in such a situation invariably play the highest card of the sequence this will inform your partner that you hold the balance of the sequence, and with this knowledge he can shape his play to suit circumstances. Supposing the King is turned up and you hold the Queen and Ten spot, when an occasion presents itself, play the Queen, and if your partner is *au fait* at the game he will know you have the Ten spot in your hand.

As a general rule, always assist when you can take two tricks.

THE LONE HAND.

There is still another privilege allowed the fortunate holder of a good hand, and that is to play it alone. If from the fulness of your hand there is a reasonable probability that you can secure all the tricks, you "play it alone," or without the assistance of your partner, and if successful are entitled to a score of four points. There is no abridgment of the right to play "alone," except when the attempt has been anticipated by your adversary's ordering it up, which a prudent player will always do in certain positions of the game, to which we shall refer with more particularity. In playing a lone hand, the following rules are now universally adopted: if the *dealer's* partner assists, or makes the trump, the *dealer* has the privilege of playing alone, or if the *eldest* hand orders up or makes the trump, *his* partner may play alone. For example:—

A and B are partners against C and D; A deals; C orders it up, and thus prevents A or B playing alone; but either C or D may play alone, provided the latter claims the privilege before C plays a card. Suppose C passes, and B assists or orders it up; neither C nor D can play alone, but B or A may, provided either claims the privilege before C plays, and C *must not play until A has discarded.* Suppose C and B both pass, D may now order up and play alone, but *neither of the others can.* Suppose C, B, and D pass, and A takes it up—of course *he* can play it alone, *but neither of the others can.* Suppose A passes, *i. e.*, turns it down, and C makes the trump; the case stands then precisely as it would have stood had he ordered up the trump first turned; and so, if C passes a second time, and B makes the trump, the case stands as it would have stood had B ordered up the turned card. If, however, C and B both pass, and D makes the trump, he may play alone, but neither of the others can. And, in like manner, if C, B, and D pass, A may make the trump, and he play alone, subject to the provision already named—that the privilege is claimed before a card is played. (*See Rule* 2.)

When the dealer's partner, having a right to go alone, elects to do so, the dealer has not the right to supersede him and play alone himself. In declaring to go alone when it his turn to settle the game and confirm, or make, the trump, as the case may be, the dealer's partner binds the adversaries, and consequently binds himself and his partner. It is not a question between the dealer and his partner, but between the partner and the opposing players. The partner, by confirming the trump and declaring to play alone, has settled the game and cut off the opponent's right who is third man. It follows that, as he has been allowed to do this, his action must at the same time have cut off the right of the dealer to change the game. It would be a change for him to substitute himself for the player who has declared to play alone. Whenever this declaration is made by a player who has the "say," it creates an obligation on the other side to play against a lone hand, and one on his part to play the lone hand. This obligation his partner cannot be permitted to break.

In playing a lone hand, it is always a great advantage to have the lead. The next advantage is, to have the last play on the first trick, therefore the eldest hand and the dealer may assume the responsibility of playing alone on a weaker hand than either of the other players.

Where a player "goes it alone," and fails to take five tricks, he is only entitled to a score of one; should he fail entirely, it entitles the adverse parties to the same score as the ordinary "Euchre," to wit, two points.

In some coteries, the adverse parties claim a score of four points upon "*Euchring*" a lone hand. We have tried to trace this principle to some authoritative source, but have failed in getting the sanction of any whose opinions are entitled to weight upon the question. (*See Decisions on Disputed Points, Euchre, Note I., page* 146.)

We have heard of instances where both sides were permitted to play alone, and in case of the failure of the original player to make a march, the other side was allowed to score four; this is, however, only a foolish innovation, directly opposed to the axiom in Euchre, viz.: that only those can play alone who legally assume the responsibility of the trump, and incur the chance of being euchred. Besides, there can be no object in playing alone against a lone player, for a Euchre *never* counts more than two. If it did, one lone player might count four in taking only three tricks, while the other must get all five tricks to count four.

There is, also, an improper custom which prevails in some parts of the West, viz.: that of giving to the player of a lone hand the privilege of the lead, irrespective and without regard to his position in the game, thus debarring the eldest hand of his right to the lead. This is so manifestly unfair that it is not worth notice here.

These and other innovations and modifications, such as *Set Back* and *Ace Euchre*, are entirely at variance with the established rules of the game, and are never played by those who are familiar with, and appreciate Euchre as a scientific amusement.

When your opponent is playing alone, and trumps a suit you or your partner leads, be sure and throw away all cards of that suit upon his subsequent leads, provided you do not have to follow suit.

When opposing a lone hand, and your partner throws away high cards of any particular suit, you may be assured that he holds good cards in some other suit; you should therefore retain to the last the highest card you hold of the suit he throws away (if you have one) in preference to any other card, unless it be an Ace of some other suit.

THE BRIDGE.

If one side stands four in the game, and the other one, such position is called a "bridge," and the following rule should be observed:

To make the theory perfectly plain, we will suppose A and B to be playing against C and D, the former being four in the game and the latter but one. C having dealt, B first looks at his hand, and finds he has but one or two small trumps; in other words, a light hand. At this stage of the game, it would be his policy to "order up" the trump, and submit to being "Euchred," in order to remove the possibility of C or D playing it alone; for if they should, by good fortune, happen to succeed, the score of four would give them the game; when, if it were ordered up, the most that could be done would be to get the Euchre, and that giving but a score of two, the next deal, with its percentage, would in all probability give A and B enough to make their remaining point and go out. If, however, B should have enough to prevent a lone hand, he can pass as usual, and await the result. The Right Bower or the Left Bower guarded is sufficient to block a lone hand.

The eldest hand is the only one who should order up at the bridge, for if he passes, his partner may rest assured that he holds commanding cards sufficient to prevent the adversaries making a lone hand. If, however, the eldest hand passes, and his partner is tolerably strong in trumps, the latter may then order up the trump to make a point and go out, for by the passing of the eldest hand his partner is informed that he holds one or more commanding trumps, and may therefore safely play for the point and game.

The eldest hand should always order up at the bridge when not sure of a trick: the weaker his hand, the greater the necessity for doing so. (*See Rule* 25.)

DISCARDING.

When the dealer takes the trump up before the play begins, it is his duty to "discard" or reject a card from his hand, in lieu of the one taken up. We will suppose the Ten of Hearts to be turned, and the dealer holds the King and Right Bower, with the Ace and Nine spot of Clubs and King of Diamonds: the proper card to reject would be the King of Diamonds, for there would be no absolute certainty of its taking a trick. The Ace might be held by the opponents, and by retaining the Ace and Nine spot of Clubs, the whole suit of Clubs might be exhausted by the Ace, and then the Nine spot might be good; or, if the trump should be one of the red suits, and the dealer held three trumps and a Seven of Spades and Seven of Hearts, it would be better to discard the Spade, for, as the dealer's strength was in the red suit, the probabilities would be that the other side would be correspondingly weak, and therefore the Heart would be better than the Spade. Where you have two of one suit and one of another to discard from, always discard the suit in which you have one card, for then you may have an opportunity to "ruff."

THE LEAD.

We have seen that the game is opened by the eldest hand leading, and much depends upon this feature of the game.

Where a dealer has been assisted, it is a common practice to lead through the assisting hand, and frequently results favorably; for, in the event of the dealer having but the trump turned, a single lead of trump, exhausts his strength, and places him at the mercy of a strong suit of lay cards. It is not, however, always advisable to "swing" a trump, for if the eldest hand holds a tenace, his duty is to manœuvre so as to secure two tricks; but this is only an exceptional case. The proper method of determining the nature of the lead is indicated by the quality of the hand and the purpose to be accomplished. The eldest hand, holding two Aces and a King, with two small trumps, of course would lead trump through assisting hand, for the reason that the only hope of securing a "Euchre" would be dependent upon the success of the lay suits, and they only can be made available after the trumps have been exhausted.

Where the dealer takes the trump voluntarily, the eldest hand is of course upon the defensive, and to lead trump under such circumstances would be disastrous.

Should your partner have the Right Bower turned, lead a small trump; by so doing, you will be sure to weaken your adversary's hand.

When your partner makes the trump, or orders it up, lead him the *best* trump you hold. Do this in any case.

When you hold the commanding cards, they should be led, to make the *march*; but if you are only strong enough to secure your point, side cards should be used; put the lowest on your partner's lead, if it be a commanding card; the highest on your adversary's.

When opposed to a lone hand, always lead the best card you have of a lay suit, so that the possibility of your partner's retaining a card of the same suit with yourself may be averted; particularly if it is a card of opposite color from the trump, for, if a red card should be trump, and an opponent played it alone, there would be more probability of his not having five red cards than of his holding that number, and the further chance, that if he did hold five red cards, it would, in like proportion, reduce the probability of your partner having one of the same suit, and give him an opportunity to weaken your opponent's hand by trumping it.

The exception to the above rule is, when you hold two or three cards of a suit, including Ace and King, and two small cards in other suits; in this case your best play would be to lead one of the latter and save your strong suit, for the reason that your partner may hold commanding cards in your weak suits, and thus you give him a chance to make a trick with them; and if this does not occur, you have your own strong suit as a reserve, and may secure a trick with it.

When playing to make a lone hand, always lead your commanding trump cards first, reserving your numerical trumps and lay suit for the closing leads. When you have exhausted your commanding trumps, having secured two tricks, and retain in your hand a numerical trump and two cards of a lay suit, lead the highest of the lay suit to make the third trick, then your trump. For instance, suppose Hearts are trumps, and you hold the Right and Left Bowers and Ten of trumps, and Ace and Nine of Spades; lead your Bowers, then the Ace of Spades, following with the Ten of trumps and your lay Nine. The reason for playing thus is obvious. You *may not* exhaust your adversaries' trumps by the first two leads, and if either of them were to retain a trump card superior to your Ten, by leading the latter you would, in all probability, suffer the mortification of being Euchered on a lone hand. For example—we will suppose one of your opponents holds the Queen, Seven, and Eight of trumps, with a small Diamond and Club, or two of either suit: he would play the two small trumps on your Bowers, and if you led the Ten of trumps, he would capture it with his Queen, and lead you a suit you could not take. Your chance of escape from such a dilemma would be very small. On the other hand, if, on your third lead, you were to lead the lay Ace, you would force your adversary to play his remaining trump, and allow you to win the point.

When you hold three small trumps and good lay cards, and desire to Euchre your opponents, lead a trump, for when trumps are exhausted you may possibly make your commanding lay cards win.

When you make the trump next in suit, always lead a trump,

unless you hold the tenace of Right Bower and Ace, and even then it would be good policy to lead the Bower, if you hold strong lay cards.

When you hold two trumps, two lay cards of the same suit, and a single lay card, lead one of the two lay cards, for you may win a trick by trumping the suit of which you hold none, and then, by leading your second lay card, you may force your opponents to trump, and thus weaken them. With such a hand it would not be good play to lead the single lay card, for you might have the good fortune to throw it away on your partner's trick, and ruff the same suit when led by your opponents.

When your partner has made or adopted the trump, it is bad play to win the lead, unless you are the fortunate possessor of a hand sufficiently strong to play for a march.

If your partner assist you, and has played a trump, and you have won a trick and the lead, do not lead him a trump unless you hold commanding cards, and are pretty certain of making the odd trick or a march, for your partner may have assisted on two trumps only, in which case such a lead would draw his remaining trump, and, in all probability, prove fatal to his most cherished plans.

When you have lost the first two tricks, and secured the third, if you hold a trump and a lay card, play the former, for, in this position of the game, it is your only chance to make or save a Euchre. There are only two exceptions to this rule, viz.: when you have assisted your partner, or when he has adopted the trump and still retains the trump card in his hand. In the former instance, you should lead the lay card, trusting to your partner to trump it; in the latter case, you should also lead the lay card, unless your trump is superior to your partner's, and your lay card is an Ace or a King, in which case you should play trump, and trust to the lay card to win the fifth trick. The reason for this play is very manifest: if your opponents hold a better trump than you, it is impossible to prevent them winning the odd trick, and, therefore, the Euchre or point; but if they hold a smaller trump, your lead exhausts it, and you may win the last trick with your lay card. This position frequently occurs in the game, and we recommend it to the attention of the novice.

ON TRUMPING.

In the game of Euchre, nothing is more important than the judicious employment of trumps, and the successful issue of the game is, perhaps, more dependent upon a thorough knowledge of their power and use, than all the other points of the game combined. In the course of this article we have already had much to say about trumps, particularly in that portion which treats of the lead, but if our readers will permit, we propose to briefly notice one subject which has remained untouched—that of trumping, or ruffing, as it is technically termed; and if our ideas on the subject will prove of any service to the tyro in the game, we shall have accomplished all we designed, both by this and other portions of the present article.

If your partner adopts or makes the trump, and you hold the Right or Left Bower alone, ruff with it as soon as you get the opportunity.

When playing second, be careful how you ruff a card of a small denomination the first time round, for it is an even chance that your partner will take the trick if you let it pass. When such a chance presents itself, throw away any single card lower than an ace, so that you may ruff the suit you throw away when it is led.

When your partner assists, and you hold a card next higher to the turn-up card, ruff with it when an opportunity occurs, for by so doing you convey valuable information to your partner.

When you are in the position of third player, ruff with high or medium trumps. This line of play forces the high trumps of the dealer, as at the game of Whist, and thereby you weaken your adversaries.

When your partner leads a lay ace, and you have none of that suit, do not trump it; but if you have a single card, throw it away upon it.

CONCLUDING HINTS.

Never lose sight of the state of the game. When you are four and four, adopt or make the trump upon a weak hand.

When the game stands three to three, hesitate before you adopt or make a trump upon a weak hand, for a Euchre will put your adversaries out.

When you are one and your opponents have scored four, you can afford to try and make it alone upon a weaker hand than if the score was more favorable to you.

When you are eldest hand and the score stands four for you and one for your opponents, do not fail to order up the trump, to prevent them from going alone. Of course you need not do this if you hold the Right Bower, or the Left Bower guarded.

Be very careful how you underplay—skilful players may attempt this, but as a general rule the tyro should take a trick when he can.

Never trump your partner's winning cards, but throw your losing and single cards upon them.

When second hand, if compelled to follow suit, head the trick if possible; this greatly strengthens your partner's game.

When you cannot follow suit or trump, dispose of your weakest card.

When opposed to a lone player, be careful how you separate two cards of the same suit. Throw away a single king rather than separate a seven and queen. Be cautious how you separate your trumps when you hold the Left Bower guarded.

When it comes your turn to say what you will do—whether you will pass, assist, order up, or go it alone—decide promptly and without unnecessary hesitation or delay. If you do not have sufficient interest in the game to give your undivided attention to it, you will do well to keep away from the table, for you have a partner's interest to consult as well as your own. Finally—lose without a murmur, and win without triumph.

We have not in this article given any other than the accepted rules, as applied to Euchre. We have at the outset stated the meaning of a few technical expressions connected with the game. We have made but few practical applications, for we have presumed that one competent to master it could apply the rules for himself.

All undertakings, whether in business or pleasure, are advantageous only as they are founded upon, and assimilated with, common sense. And until the player unites reason with fortune, he can never count with any degree of certainty upon success.

The innumerable phases which the game is capable of assuming would require more paper and words to express than one would willingly devote to pleasure. For when the pursuit of pastime merges into the exactions of study, relaxation becomes a task, and "desire fails."

TWO-HANDED EUCHRE.

In this, as in the four-handed game, the deal being made, the non-dealer may pass or order up; should he pass, the dealer, at his option, may pass, or discard and take up the trump, when the game begins by the lead of the non-dealer; but should the dealer think his hand not strong enough to risk a play, he too will pass, when his adversary may pass again, or make a trump (which, as a general rule, should be next in suit); if he pass a second time, the dealer has the right to make a trump or again pass, in which case the cards are to be bunched, and the deal passed to the original non-dealer.

If the dealer takes up the trump and plays the hand, he must win three tricks to make a point; or should he take the five tricks, he makes a "march," which entitles him to score two points. Should he fail to make three tricks, he is Euchred and his adversary counts two points. The same rules apply to the party ordering up, or making the trump.

In passing, or ordering up, much will depend upon the state of the game, and what the player desires to accomplish; he may pass upon a good hand, when he has reason to believe that by so doing he will Euchre his adversary, should he play the hand. In this case, too, he should have good reason to suppose that his adversary will take up the trump, or else have cards to make the trump himself.

The player, remembering that he has but a single hand to contend against, may play, or even order up, if he has a reasonable hope of making three tricks.

Lead your strongest trumps first, until you have won two tricks, and then, having a trump left, lead some other card, so that, if your adversary takes it, you may have a chance to trump the card he leads, and thus make your point. Having won two tricks, and your adversary being without a trump, play for a *march*, by leading trumps, or your highest cards.

The deal is considered equal to a point, therefore never pass the deal unless to save a Euchre.

Having discarded, you have no right to take the card back and discard another, even though you have made a mistake. Your opponent must profit by your mistakes, as well as by your bad play, or weak hand.

THREE-HANDED EUCHRE.

This game, as its name indicates, is played by three persons, and as each one plays for himself, and is therefore opposed by two adversaries, the game requires closer attention, and the exercise of more judgment than any of the other Euchre games.

In two-handed Euchre, the player may stand upon a slight hand, but not so in this game; to stand or order up he must have a good hand, inasmuch as he has two hands combined against him, and should he be Euchred, both adversaries count two.

Another important feature of the game is, that the play varies according to the stage of the game; for example—at the beginning of the game, each player strives to make all he can for himself; at the first play the dealer makes a *march*, and counts two; the next dealer makes one point, and the third dealer two; the first dealer again deals, and makes one point; the game now stands thus:—

> Dealer No. 1........................3 points.
> " 2............................1 point.
> " 3............................2 points.

No. 2 now has the deal, and should he be Enchered, No. 1 wins the game; therefore, while No. 1 plays to win the game by a Euchre, No. 3 plays to let the dealer make a point, or even a march, which would make the game stand—

> No. 1........................3 points.
> " 2........................3 points.
> " 3........................2 points.

It is now No. 3's deal, and if the circumstances justify the case, both his adversaries may combine against him and Euchre him, if they can, which would put them both out; or, they may both play so as to let him make a point, that each may have another chance to win the game. Each player is now three, and No. 1 deals—but as they are all anxious to win the game, without dividing the honor or the profit, the dealer is permitted to make one point, but not two, if his opponents can prevent it.

No. 2 next strives to win by a march, but, as in the last case, his adversaries play to prevent his making more than one point; and the same strife again takes place when No. 3 deals.

Now, as each player is four, the game must terminate with the next deal, so that the dealer must either make his point or be Euchred, in which case both his adversaries win, and therefore on the last deal, both non-dealers play the strength of their combined game against the common enemy, and thus beat him, if they can. The dealer, however, has a remedy against a defeat, which is in this: if, upon examining his hand, he believes he cannot make a point, he can pass, and thus throw the deal elsewhere, thus having one more chance to win, and the same policy may be pursued by each player, until the game is played out. In some coteries the player who achieves a march is entitled to score three points, for the reason that three persons are engaged in the game; but thus counting three may be considered an innovation, and not the regular game. Where parties differ in opinion as to the right to score three, the question should be settled before the game is commenced.

SET-BACK EUCHRE.

This game may be played by two or more persons, and is governed by the same rules as ordinary Euchre, except in the matter of counting, as hereinafter explained. It is quite amusing and exciting, especially when played for money.

Suppose four persons sit down to play, and agree that the pool shall be one dollar: each one contributes twenty-five cents. At the beginning of the game, each player is five, and now the struggle commences to wipe out these scores, and thus win the game. Each player plays for himself, and all are combined against him who orders up or plays the hand. Should any one not win a single trick, he has one point added to his score, and whoever is euchred is obliged to put another quarter into the pool, and has two points added to his score.

The player who thinks he cannot take a trick, has the right to throw up his hand, and thus save himself from being *set back*. The player who is the first to reduce his score to nothing, wins the game and the pool.

The above is the game of Set-Back Euchre pure and simple, but various modifications are frequently introduced. The following are the most popular of these:—

After a trump is made, ordered up, or taken up, should any player deem himself possessed of a sufficient force of trumps to make a march, he will say, "I declare"—which signifies he will play to take all the tricks—and if he is successful in making the march, he wins the game and pool, no matter how many points are scored against him. Should he, however, be unsuccessful in the undertaking, he forfeits double the number of points against him, and, in addition, must pay in the pool the penalty of a Euchre. For instance, if a player stands with seven points to go, and *declares* without making the march, he must be "set back" to fourteen points, and pay a quarter to the pool. The player who declares to make a march has the privilege of the lead, and becomes eldest hand, unless he be the dealer; but if the dealer declares, he does not have that privilege. In some circles it is customary for the unsuccessful players to pay to the winner of the pool a certain sum (previously agreed upon) for each point they have to go when the game is concluded; this is not, however, considered a rule to be strictly followed, but may be left to the option of the players.

Another variety of this game is played as follows: When the party adopting, making, or ordering up the trump, is Euchred he is set back two points, while his adversary scores two, as in the ordinary game. The severity of the penalty for a Euchre, in this game, being so great, unusual caution should be observed in taking up or making a trump, especially as each man plays for himself, and is therefore opposed by all the other players, as in the three-handed game, the laws of which apply with equal force to this.

LAP, SLAM, JAMBONE, AND JAMBOREE.

By whom these variations were invented is unknown, but it is generally conceded that they are of Southern origin, where Euchre has long been a decided favorite, and where these variations are more frequently played, than in any other part of our country.

LAP.

The *Lap* game may be played by two, three, or four persons, when they agree to play a series of games, so that the *lap* may be applied, which is simply counting upon the score of the ensuing game all the points made over and above the five of which the game consists. For example, if one party, having made four points, should Euchre his opponents, or make a march, either of which entitles him to score two points, he not only wins the game then being played, but counts one point on the next game ; or, if a player in a four-handed game, having four points, plays a lone hand, and makes his five tricks, he wins the game and scores three points on the next game. When the lap game is played, it is usual to count four points when a lone hand is Euchred.

SLAM, OR LOVE-GAME.

Slam and *Love* appear to be synonymous terms, and, when applied to games, imply that when a party has won a game before his opponent has made a single point, the vanquished has been *Slamed*, or played a Love-game. The term *Love* is used in all games, and simply means nothing. In billiards, the professional marker or keeper of the game announces, at the end of each count, the state of the game, thus—twenty-five-love—meaning that one player is twenty-five and the other nothing. In Euchre, the penalty for being *slamed* is, that the game thus lost is to be counted a double game, and must be counted as two games. And further, suppose a player, being four, and his adversaries nothing, plays a lone hand and makes his five tricks, he not only wins that game, which is to be counted as two games, but counts the extra three points on the score of the third game, by means of the Lap as heretofore explained.

JAMBONE.

Jambone is a word unknown to Webster, but, as applied to Euchre, means that a party who plays Jambone plays a lone hand with his cards exposed upon the table. Thus, if a player holds what he supposes to be an invincible hand, with which he cannot fail to win five tricks, announces in his turn that he will play Jambone, he spreads his cards upon the table face up. When the cards are thus exposed, the player entitled to the lead has the right to call any one of the cards so exposed to be played to the first trick, but this right does not extend to any but the party entitled to lead. Let us illustrate by a single example :—

Suppose the dealer turns up as the trump card the King of Hearts. The other players pass, or his partner may propose to assist—but, upon examining his cards, he finds he holds the two red Bowers, the Ace and Ten of trumps, and a card of some other suit, and thereupon determines to risk a Jambone, which he announces, and exposes his cards, having discarded the odd card. The eldest hand, or player entitled to the lead, holds the Queen of trumps, plays it, and calls for the Ten, which the dealer is obliged to play, thus losing the trick. Although he wins the other four tricks, he can count only one point; but should it so happen that the Jambone player, under all the disadvantages of exposing his hand, and of giving the elder hand the right to call for either of his cards, as explained, wins all the tricks, he is entitled to count eight points.

The right to the *call* is forfeited when the partner of the player having the lead gives any intimation which enables the two to win the first trick.

A Jambone hand may be played by either party, subject to the same rules which govern playing alone in the regular game.

When the adverse party order up or make the trump, a Jambone hand cannot be played, and the holder must be content with the satisfaction of Euchring his opponent.

The Jambone player being entitled to lead, his left-hand opponent only, has the right to say which of the exposed cards shall be lead.

No *call* can be made after the first trick has been played, after which the Jambone player may exercise his own judgment, and lead whichever card he pleases.

If the Jambone player wins less than five tricks, he can score but one point; and should he fail to win three tricks, his adversaries are entitled to score eight points.

When the dealer plays Jambone, and the eldest hand leads a card not a trump, but which the dealer will trump, he should call for the lowest exposed card, so that his partner may have a chance to play a higher trump than the one called, and thus win the trick.

If the dealer holding a Jambone hand finds that by discarding and taking up the trump, he weakens his hand, he is not obliged to discard, so that the turn-up card merely indicates the trump suit.

The player calling the card for the first trick, must call it the moment he leads, or he forfeits his right to the call.

If the lead belongs to the Jambone player, his opponent entitled to the call must call before a card is played, otherwise the Jambone player may play any card he chooses, the right to the call being forfeited.

These are the most important points in the Jambone game, which the player will find quite interesting, and which will call forth his greatest skill and the exercise of his profoundest judgment.

JAMBOREE.

Jamboree signifies the combination of the five highest cards, as, for example, the two Bowers, Ace, King, and Queen of trumps in one hand, which entitles the holder to count *sixteen* points. The holder of such a hand, simply announces the fact, as no play is necessary; but should he play the hand as a Jambone, he can count only eight points, whereas he could count sixteen if he played it, or announced it as a Jamboree.

When the parties are playing Laps and Slams, and one of the players has four points to his opponent's nothing, and announces a Jamboree, the sixteen points thus won, added to his four, making twenty points, is equal to four games, each of them a Slam, which entitles him to count eight games in all.

Jamboree, like Jambone, cannot be played as such, if the adverse party order up the trump or make it, in which case the hand can only make two points, as in an ordinary Euchre.

CRIBBAGE.

Of the origin of Cribbage we are not aware that any thing is known further than that it is essentially an English game.

The game is played with a full pack of fifty-two cards: Sixty-one points constitutes the game. These points are scored on a Cribbage Board, of which see a representation on next page. It has, as will be seen, sixty-one holes, and in these the points aforesaid are marked; the whole table being subdivided into compartments of five holes each.

The board is placed either across or lengthways between the players. It is a matter of indifference how the end of the board from which you commence is placed; but you must count from that end which contains the sixty-first, or game hole; beginning at the outside edge (A or B), and passing along it to the top, then down the inside row to game. To mark the game, each player has two pegs; if the first score be two, stick a peg and leave it in the second hole, and when next it becomes your turn to mark, place the other peg in the number that gives the points you have to mark, counting from your first peg. When you have to mark a third score, take out the back peg, and reckon from the foremost, which must never be disturbed during the progress of the game, the scores being invariably marked by the hindmost peg of the two. Thus, the foremost peg always keeping its hole, the players can detect the amount that is marked, and check each other's score. To avoid confusion, it is usual for the pegs of each party to be of different colors; although the one player never, in any way, touches his adversary's half of the board.

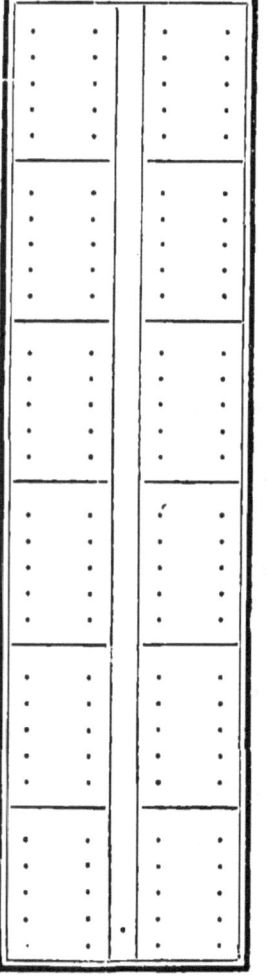

A Game Hole. B

All the Kings, Queens, Knaves, and Tens, count as ten each; the rest of the cards according to their ordinary value, as Sixes for six, Eights for eight, and so forth; Aces reckon one only. This means merely their value as cards. The points which count for the game are made by Fifteens, Sequences, Flushes, Pairs, &c.

There are games at Cribbage for two, three, or four players; but the theory is contained in Five-card Cribbage for two players.

FIVE-CARD CRIBBAGE.

The players shuffle the cards in the usual manner, and cut for deal. The player cutting the lowest card deals. The lowest card in cutting is always the Ace; but in Cribbage, if two Court Cards, or a Court Card and a Ten, are cut, there is a tie, and the players must cut again. The deal determined, the cards are shuffled by the dealer, who then lays them on the table on his opponent's side of the Cribbage-board, which is usually placed on the table between the players. The non-dealer then cuts the pack into two parts; and with the undermost half the dealer distributes five cards each, beginning with his adversary. The dealer then places the remaining cards on the other heap, and the pack remains undisturbed by either party till the crib cards are discarded. Each player then looks at his hand, and throws out two cards, it being imperative that the non-dealer throws first. The elder hand (the non-dealer) then again cuts the cards on the table by taking up any number, not fewer than three, without exposing the faces of any of the cards; the dealer lifts the topmost card of the lot left on the table, the non-dealer replaces the cards he cut, and the dealer puts the top card, face upward, on the whole. This operation, though rather complicated in description, is very simple in practice. The discarded and the exposed cut-card (the turn-up) form what is called the *crib*. The number scored in the crib belongs always to the dealer; the deal being taken alternately. If a Knave happen to be the "turn-up," the dealer takes "two for his heels." The turn-up is reckoned in making up the score of each player's hand, as well as of the crib.

The game then commences. The elder hand plays a card—on his own side of the Cribbage-board—calling out the value of the card played. Thus, we will suppose the elder hand to hold a King, Knave, and a Five; and the dealer, a Seven, Knave, and Eight; and that a Four has been turned up. The non-dealer then plays (say) the Knave, and says, "Ten;" the dealer replies by playing his Knave, and cries "Twenty," and takes two for the pair; his opponent then plays his King, and says "Thirty." This being the nearest point to thirty-one, and the dealer having no Ace in his hand, cries "Go," when his adversary scores one hole on the board. Each player's hand is then counted; the elder scoring four—two for each fifteen; and the dealer two, for the seven and eight, which make fifteen. But if the Knave in either hand be of the same suit as the turn-up, the holder of such Knave scores "one for his nob." The crib is then taken by the dealer, and the game proceeds as before. Or, to explain this more fully: after dealing, laying for crib, and cutting, as explained, the elder hand plays a card, which the other endeavors to pair or fifteen—the pips on the one card being added to those on the other. Then the non-dealer plays another card, and so on up to thirty-one, or the nearest point to it. For the "go" a single hole is scored, except when exactly thirty-one is made, when two holes are added to the score of the player whose last card makes the required number.

The points which each party has made, during the playing out the hand, having been all taken at the time they were gained, and the deal being finished, each party now completes his score, and marks that number of points towards game to which he is entitled. The non-dealer reckons first; and, having marked his gains, if any, on the board, the dealer in his turn counts—first, his hand, and then his crib, for the crib belongs to the dealer.

The hands are reckoned thus, in every way that it is possible to produce the combination:

	Points.
For every fifteen—as, 7 and 8; 10 and 5; 9 and 6; 8, 3, and 4, &c.,	2
For a sequence of three or four cards—as, 2, 3, 4, 5,	3 or 4
For a flush in hand, that is, three cards of any one suit,	3
For a full flush, when the cards in hand and the turn-up are of the same suit,	4
For a pair (two of a kind, as two Fives, Sixes, Sevens, &c.),	2
For a pair-royal (three of a sort),	6
For a double pair-royal (four of a kind, as four Kings, Aces, &c.),	12
Knave of the suit turned up (the nob),	1

Sequences always count double when, in the four cards, there are two of a sort. Thus: suppose the hand to consist of a Seven, an Eight, and two Nines, the score would be ten—two for the fifteen (7 and 8), and six for the double sequence, 7, 8, 9; 7, 8, 9; with two for the pair of Nines. Or, again, suppose the hand to consist of a Three, a Four, and two Fives, the score would be—

```
        3 4 5  -  -  -  -  -  -   3 holes ⎫
        3 4 5  -  -  -  -  -  -   3   "   ⎬ 8 holes
        The pair -  -  -  -  -  - 2   "   ⎭
```

The non-player, at the commencement of the game, takes three holes as an equivalent for the crib belonging to the dealer. This "three for non-deal" may be taken at any part of the game, but it is usual, in order to avoid confusion, to take them at the beginning.

After counting up all the points another deal then takes place, and is conducted in a similar manner; and so on, until either one of the parties has completed the required number of sixty-one, when he is proclaimed the victor, and the game is finished.

In reckoning the hand and crib, after the deal, you have been already informed that the non-dealer counts first. It will facilitate your reckoning, if you sum up the amount of points to which you are entitled, in the following order: Firstly, Fifteens; secondly,

Sequences; thirdly, Flushes; fourthly, Pairs, Pairs-Royal, or Double Pairs-Royal; fifthly, the point for the Knave. Reckoning up the hand, or crib, is technically termed "showing." Thus the non-dealer is said to have "the first show," a point of immense importance at the final stage of the game; since he may thus be enabled just to "show out," and consequently win the game; while the dealer may hold in his hand, and crib, points enough to make him out three times over, but altogether useless, since he has not the first show.

The non-dealer having summed up his score, under the observation of his opponent, the latter then performs the same operation, as relates to his own hand. He then turns up crib, which has up to this time lain *perdue*, and scores all to which it may entitle him.

Cribbage differs from all other games at cards by the almost numberless varieties of chances it affords. In almost all the books on card-games, cribbage is said to be useful to young people in accustoming them to calculate readily. We may perhaps take this with the least possible grain of salt. Let us now explain the principal

TECHNICAL TERMS USED IN CRIBBAGE.

Crib.—The two cards thrown from the hand of each player. These, with the turn-up, form the dealer's crib.

Fifteens.—Every two, three, or more cards which, added together, make fifteen, reckon two holes towards game, whether they be made in play, hand, or crib. Fifteens may be formed of court cards and Fives, Tens and Fives, Nines and Sixes, Eights and Sevens, or by three or four cards together. Thus, a hand consisting of three Fours with a Three turned up would count eight—a fifteen and a pair-royal; a hand of a Nine and three Sixes would count twelve—three fifteens and a pair-royal. Or, 7, 7, 4, 4, eight points—two fifteens and two pairs; or a crib of 7, 7, 7, 7 and 1 on the pack, would score 24—six fifteens and a double pair-royal. Or a crib consisting of four Deuces and a Nine turn-up, 20—fifteen 8 and 12 for pair-royal, and so on *ad infinitum*. This method of counting fifteens is common to all games at Cribbage. Whenever fifteen can be made of two, three, or more cards, in play or hand, the player making the fifteen adds two points to his score.

Pair or Pairs.—Every pair made in the play or the hand, reckons for two points. To pair is to play a card of the same description, but it need not be of the same suit. If a tenth card be played, and you can answer it immediately with a similar tenth card, without exceeding thirty-one, it is a pair, and counts two. But in these pairs, all tenth cards do not count alike. It must be King for King, Queen for Queen, and so forth. At the end of the deal, you take the turn-up card to assist you in pairing, and count two for all pairs made by its assistance.

Pair-Royal or Prial. This consists of three cards of a similar sort, held either in the hand or crib, or occurring in the course of the game, as three Kings, three Aces, three Nines, &c. It scores six. Thus: if the leader play a Six, you put another Six on it, and score two for the pair; he then returns a Six, makes a pair-royal, and counts six points. If you have a pair-royal in your hand or your crib, you also score Six for it; and should you only hold a pair, and turn up the third, it reckons also for six. It is needless to say these combinations do not count for points, when other cards have been played between them.

Double Pair-Royal. Four cards of a sort make this combination, for which the score is twelve; alike, whether made in play, or in the hand, or in the crib. The turn-up card reckons with hand and crib, in this, as in every other case. Moreover, should your opponent have made a pair-royal, by playing a third of a sort, you are entitled to the double pair-royal, if you answer him with a fourth.

In taking six for a pair-royal, or twelve for a double pair-royal, you are not to suppose that the six and the twelve are merely increased numbers, bestowed as premiums for such combinations of the cards, and settled by arbitrary arrangement, independent of the rule that two points are allowed for every pair. A pair reckons for two, and the same principle, applied to a pair-royal, produces six; because, as a pair-royal contains three distinct pairs, you score two for each pair. Place, for instance, three Sixes in a row on the table, and mark them 1, 2, and 3, thus:

1	2	3
Six	Six	Six

Here Nos. 1 and 2 form the first pair, Nos. 1 and 3 the second pair, and Nos. 2 and 3 the third pair; without the same two cards having ever been reckoned more than once together.

Having analyzed this example, there will be little difficulty in

TECHNICAL TERMS. 91

ascertaining the number of pairs to be found by *taking in pieces* a double pair-royal. The readiest way to attain demonstration is to place the four Sixes in a row on the table, as you did the three Sixes, and number them 1, 2, 3, and 4, thus:

1	2	3	4
Six	Six	Six	Six

Nos. 1 and 2 combined together, form a pair, and yield
two points, for which carry out - - - - 2
Nos. 1 and 3 form the second pair, and give two more 2
Nos. 1 and 4 form the third pair - - - - 2
Nos. 2 and 3 form the fourth pair - - - - 2
Nos. 2 and 4 form the fifth pair - - - - 2
Nos. 3 and 4 form the sixth pair - - - - 2
                                      Total - - - - 12

Thus, we have six distinct pairs in a double pair-royal, which, of course, are thereby entitled to twelve points. Observe, that in making these points, although we reckon the cards over and over again, they always unite in different associations, and the same two cards are never reckoned twice together.

Sequences consist of three or more cards following in successive numbers, whether of the same suit or otherwise. He who holds them scores one point for every card in the combination, whether it take place in playing or in counting the hand or crib. But there cannot be a sequence under three cards. As in certain other cases, the court cards, King, Queen, and Knave, rank in sequences, after their usual classification as to rank, and not all alike as tenth cards. To form a sequence in play, it matters not which of the cards is played first or last, provided the sequence can be produced by a transposition of the order in which they fell. Thus, you lead the Five of Hearts, your adversary returns the Three of Diamonds; you then play the Four of any suit, and score three for the sequence; he then plays Six and makes four, and so on, as long as the continuous sequence can be made. The spirit of this rule may be applied to all combinations occurring in regular successions.

You here observe that it does not matter of what suit are the cards forming the sequence, nor does the order signify in which they are played. You must not pass thirty-one in making a sequence. If

4*

a sequence in play is once broken, it must be formed afresh, or can not be acted on.

In reckoning your sequences at the close of the deal, you use the card turned up along with your hand and crib; and reckon them every way they will. A single example of this will here suffice:—

Suppose the crib to consist of two Kings (Clubs and Diamonds), and two Queens (Hearts and Spades), the Knave of Spades being the card turned up;—how many can you take for sequences?

Twelve, being four sequences of three each; to be computed by reckoning the Knave with the Kings and Queens; ringing the changes in the latter somewhat in a similar manner to the mode in which you have been taught to form a double pair-royal. To simplify this, take the Knave, the two Queens, and the two Kings, and spread them before you; when they will count thus:—

Knave, with Queen of Hearts and King of Clubs	3
Knave, with Queen of Spades and King of Clubs	3
Knave, with Queen of Hearts and King of Diamonds	3
Knave, with Queen of Spades and King of Diamonds	3
Points for four Sequences	12

A Flush.—A Flush cannot happen in play, but occurs only in computing the hand or crib. A Flush signifies that all the cards in hand or crib are of the same suit, in which case you are allowed to mark one point for every card of which the Flush is composed. Thus, if your hand comprise three Hearts, you will take, on scoring for your hand, three for the flush in Hearts; and should the turn-up card chance to be also a Heart, you will add another point for that, making four altogether. You are not permitted, however, to reckon a flush in the crib, unless the cards, of which the crib is composed, are of the same suit as the card turned up. It is essential to recollect the difference between a flush in the hand and a flush in the crib.

His Nob.—The Knave of the turned-up suit. In counting, in hand or crib, it marks one point.

His Heels.—The Knave when turned up. It reckons for two holes, but is only once counted.

End Hole.—The last hole on the board into which the player places his peg when he makes game.

Pegs.—The little brass, wooden or ivory pieces with which the game is scored on the board.

The Go.—The point nearest thirty-one. If thirty-one exactly be made, the player scores two holes; for the simple "go," one hole: in addition, of course, to any more he may make with his last card.

Last.—The three holes taken by the non-dealer at Five-card Cribbage.

The Start.—The state of the pack after being cut and before the cards are dealt.

RULES OF CRIBBAGE.

1. The players cut for deal, the holder of the lowest card being dealer. The Ace is lowest, and all ties cut again. All tenth cards —Kings, Queens, Knaves, and Tens—are ties.

2. Faced cards necessitate a new deal, if called for by the non-dealer.

[In the old laws, a faced card in the dealer's hand was considered of no consequence: but according to modern play, any card faced in the process of dealing obliges a new deal; but there is no penalty attached to the mistake.]

3. Should too many cards be dealt to either, the non-dealer may score two, and demand another deal, if the error be detected previous to his taking up his cards; if he do not wish a new deal, the top or last-dealt cards may be withdrawn and packed; when any player has more than the proper number of cards in hand, the opponent may score four, and call a new deal.

[This is seldom enforced—a new deal following any misdeal.]

4. If a player touch the pack after dealing, till the period of cutting it for the turn-up card, his opponent may score two points.

5. If a player take more than he is entitled to, the other party not only puts him back as many points as are overscored, but likewise takes the same extra number for his own game.

[This is called "pegging." You must be careful how you peg your opponent. If he has taken too many holes, the proper way to rectify his error, whether it be wilful or otherwise, is to take your back peg and place it in the hole his front peg should have properly occupied. Then remove his front peg, and make it your front peg by adding as many to your score as he has wrongfully taken. If in pegging him you remove his or your own front peg first, he may claim to have the pegs as they were; or if you peg him wrongly, he is entitled to score all the holes he formerly marked, and your error in addition.]

6. Should either player even meddle with his own pegs unnecessarily, the opponent may score two points; and if either take out his front peg, he must place the same back behind the other. If any peg be misplaced by accident, a bystander may replace it, ac-

cording to the best of his judgment; but the bystander should never otherwise interfere unless requested by the players.

7. If any player neglect to set up what he is entitled to, he loses the points so omitted to be taken, but his adversary cannot add them to his own score.

[Formerly the opponent could add to his own score all holes omitted to be taken; but this is now obsolete; the original loss being sufficient penalty.]

8. Each player may place his own cards, when the deal is concluded, upon the pack.

9. The cards are to be dealt one by one.

[It was formerly the custom in six and eight-card cribbage to deal two, three, or four at a time. The rule now-a-days, however, is as we have given it for all games at cribbage.]

10. The non-dealer, at the commencement of the game, in five-card cribbage, scores three points, called *three for last;* but in six and eight-card cribbage this is not to be done.

11. After the score is taken on the board, the pegs must not be replaced, if a mistake be perceived, without the consent of the opponent.

12. Neither player is allowed to touch his adversary's pegs, under penalty of losing his game, except it be to peg him for a wrong score.

13. All cases of dispute must be decided by appeal to the bystanders.

14. Three cards at least must be removed from the pack in cutting for deal or turn-up.

15. When the Knave is turned up, "two for his heels" must be taken before a card is played, or the two cannot be scored.

16. The non-dealer discards for the crib first, and a card once laid out cannot be recalled if it be covered.

17. Neither player may touch the crib cards till the hand is played out.

[It is usual to throw the crib cards over to the dealer's side of the board, which plan insures regularity, and indicates whose deal it is. The pack is also placed on the other side ready for the next dealer.]

18. The dealer shuffles the cards, and the non-dealer cuts them for "the start." In four-handed cribbage, the left-hand adversary shuffles, and the right-hand adversary cuts.

MAXIMS FOR LAYING OUT THE CRIB.

Much of the success of the cribbage player depends on the manner he lays out his cards for crib. The player should consider not only his own hand, but also to whom the crib belongs, as well as the state of the game; for what might be proper in one situation would be highly imprudent in another.

Firstly, When it is NOT your own crib, you will lay out such cards as are likely to be, in an average number of cases, of the least possible advantage to your opponent, in the production of pairs, fifteens, sequences, &c.

Secondly, When it is your own crib, you will lay out favorable cards for the crib.

Thirdly, It being your own crib to which you are about to discard, you will prefer consulting the interests of the crib, in preference even to those of your hand.

The most advantageous cribbage cards are Fives, Sevens, Eights, &c., when so assorted as to form fifteens, sequences, pairs, or flushes. The Five is, of all others, the most useful card, since it makes fifteen equally with either one of the tenth cards; of which there are no fewer than sixteen in the pack. Fives must therefore be in general the most eligible cards to lay out to your own crib, and the least eligible (for you) to lay out to your adversary; since, in so doing, you are almost certain to give him points. To discard a pair of any cards, again, is mostly bad play, unless it is for your own crib; and cards which follow each other in order, as a Three and Four, or Nine and Ten, being likely to be brought in for sequences, are generally bad cards to lay out in the case of its being your adversary's crib. The same calculation should, in its principle, be carried out as far as possible. Suppose you discard, to your opponent's crib, two Hearts, when you might with equal propriety have laid out a Heart and a Club instead,—you here give him the chance, however remote you may fancy it, of making a flush in his crib, which could not be effected by him, had you laid out the Heart and Club.

To lay out cards purposely, which are disadvantageous for the crib, is called in the "cribbage dialect" of our ancestors "balking' or "bilking" the crib.

The least likely cards to reckon for points in the crib, and therefore generally the best to discard for your adversary, are Kings; since a sequence can only be made up to, or as it may be termed, on one side of them; and cannot be carried beyond them. A King is therefore a greater balk in the crib than the Queen. So, again, of an Ace,— a sequence can only be made from it, and not up to it; and an Ace is therefore frequently a great balk to a crib; though in discarding an Ace some judgment is required to be exercised, being often a good card to hold for play; and forming a component part of fifteen, particularly when combined with Sixes, Sevens, and Eights, or with Fours and Tenth cards.

The cards, then, best adapted to balk our antagonist's crib, are a King, with a Ten, Nine, Eight, Seven, Six, or Ace; a Queen, with a Nine, Eight, Seven, Six, or Ace, or cards equally distinct or far off, and therefore certain not to be united in sequence by meeting with any other cards whatever. Of course, particular hands require particular play, and general principles must give way before their exceptions. "Circumstances alter cases;" throughout this work, as in all similar works, the author writes for what may be called "average hands of cards," and recommends that play which would be most conducive to success in the largest proportion of events.

Never lay out a Knave for your adversary's crib, if you can with propriety avoid it, as the probability of the turn-up card being of the same suit as the Knave is three to one against it. Consequently, it is only three to one but the retaining such Knave in your hand gains you a point; whereas, should you discard it to your opponent's crib, it is only three to one against the chance of its making him a point; hence the probable difference of losing a point by throwing out your Knave is only three to two and one-third; or nine to seven; that is to say, in laying out a Knave for your antagonist's crib, when you could equally keep the same in your hand, sixteen times, you give away just seven points; it being only nine to seven but you give away a point every time you play in this manner, and every single point is of consequence if contending against a good player. As we just now remarked, there may, of course, occur exceptions to this and every other rule.

The cards which are usually the best to lay out for your own crib are two Fives, Five and Six, Five and Tenth card, Three and Two, Seven and Eight, Four and Ace, Nine and Six. and similar couples. If you have no similar cards to lay out, put down

MAXIMS FOR LAYING OUT THE CRIB.

as close cards as you can; because, by this means you have the greater chance of either being assisted by the cards laid out by your adversary, or by the turn-up; and further, you should uniformly lay out two cards of the same suit for your own crib, in preference, *cæteris paribus*, to two other cards of the same kind, that are of different suits, as this gives you the probable chance of flushing your crib; whereas, should you lay out two cards of different suits, all gain under the head of a flush is at once destroyed. It is mostly good play to retain a sequence in hand, in preference to cards less closely connected; more especially should such sequence be a flush; and once more remember, that the probable chance of points from the crib is something nearly approaching to twenty per cent. over the hand. It is, therefore, indispensably your duty, if you wish to win, to give the lead to your crib at the expense of your hand.

In general, whenever you are able to hold a pair-royal in hand, you should lay out the other two cards, both for your own and your adversaries' crib—some few cases, however, excepted. For example, should you hold a pair-royal of any description, along with two Fives, it would be highly dangerous to give your antagonist the brace of Fives, unless in such a situation of the game that your pair-royal would make you certainly out, having the first show, or else that your adversary is so nearly home himself that the contents of the crib are wholly unimportant. Many other cards are very hazardous to lay out to your adversary's crib, even though you can hold a pair-royal—such as Two and Three, Five and Six, Seven and Eight, and Five and tenth card; therefore, should you have such cards combined together, you must pay particular regard to the stage of the game. This caution equally applies to many other cards, and particularly when, the game being nearly over, it happens to be your own deal, and that your opponent is nearly home, or within a moderate show-out. Here, then, should be especial care taken to retain in hand cards which may enable you to play "off" or wide of your adversary, and thus prevent his forming any sequence or pair-royal. In similar positions you should endeavor, also, to keep cards that will enable you to have a good chance of winning the end hole, which frequently saves a game.

HOW TO PLAY THE HIGH GAME.

The chances in this game are often so great, that even between skilful players, it is possible, at Five-card Cribbage, when the adversary is fifty-six, for a lucky player, who had not previously made a single hole, to be more than up in two deals, his opponent getting no farther than sixty in that time; and in Four-handed Cribbage a case may occur, wherein neither of the two players hold a single point in hand, and yet the dealer and his friend, with the assistance of a Knave turned up, may make sixty-one by play in one deal, while the adversaries only get twenty-four; and although this may not happen for many years, yet similar games may now and then be met with.

The following we take from Walker's treatise, as quoted by all the modern writers on the game.

"Should you hold a Three and a Two, it is frequently the best play to lead off the Three (or the Two), on the chance of your adversary playing a tenth card (*of which never forget that there are sixteen*), making thirteen, when your Two (or your Three) drops in, making two points for the fifteen. The same principle applies to the leading from a Four and an Ace, and has this additional advantage, that should you thus succeed in forming fifteen, your opponent can form no sequence from your cards.

"Remember, that when your adversary leads a Seven or Eight, should you make a fifteen, you give him the chance of coming in with a Six or a Nine, and thus gaining three holes against you; but this will sometimes tend to your advantage by allowing of your rejoinder with a fourth card in sequence. For instance, your opponent leads an Eight, and you make fifteen by answering with a Seven; he plays a Six, making twenty-one, and scores three for the sequence, but having a Nine or Ten, you play it, and score four or two after him. In all such cases, play to the state of your game; for what would be at one time correct, would be, at another, the worst possible play.

"To lead from a pair is generally safe play, good; because, should your opponent pair you, you form a pair-royal, making six holes; while the chance of his rejoining with a fourth is too small to be taken into consideration. It would rarely, though, be correct to lead from a pair of Fives, as he would make fifteen with a Tenth card.

"When your adversary leads a card which you can pair, it is better to make fifteen, in preference to the pair, should you be able so to do; as you will naturally suspect he wishes you to pair him, in order to make a pair-royal himself. But here, as elsewhere, your chief guide is the relative state of the game.

"When you can possibly help it, consistently with your cards, do not, in play, make the number twenty-one; for your antagonist is then likely to come in with a tenth card, and score two.

"Should you hold a Nine and Three, it is good play to lead the Three; because, should it be paired, you form fifteen by playing the Nine. The same applies to the holding of a Four and a Seven; in which case, should your Four be paired, you make fifteen with the Seven.

"The following style of play facilitates your obtaining the end hole. Should you hold two low cards and one high card, lead the former; but should you hold one low card and two high cards, lead from the latter. Like other general directions, all this is, however, subject to contingencies.

"Holding a Ten and Five, and two holes being at the moment an object of great importance, lead the tenth card, in hopes of your adversary's making fifteen, when you can pair his Five.

"Holding a Seven and Four, it is good play to lead the Four; because, if paired, your Seven comes in for fifteen: the same direction applies to your holding a Six and Three, and Three and Nine, or other cards similarly related.

"When compelled to lead from a sequence of three cards, play the lowest, or highest, in preference to the middle card. With a Six, Seven, and Eight, the Seven is, however, then the best card, as it enables you to bring in a sequence.

"In laying out for your own crib, suppose you hold a pair of Fives, and no tenth card, discard them both. Bear in mind that of all the tenth cards, the Knave is of the most importance; and that those cards which tell best in counting the hand, are not always the best for playing.

"If in play you throw down a Four, making the number twenty-seven, your adversary has the chance of pairing your Four, and of making at the same time thirty-one. If you make twenty-eight with a Three, you incur the same risk. These apparent trifles must be studied, and similar points on your part, if possible, avoided, while you should be constantly on the watch to grasp them for yourself, should your antagonist leave an opening.

"As the dealer plays last, his chances are greater than those of the leader for making the end hole or other desirable points in play. The dealer has also in his favor the chance of gaining the two points by lifting a Knave or Jack, and making 'two for his heels.'"

The phrase "playing off" is used in contradiction to its reverse, "playing on." Thus, should your adversary lead a Five, and you follow with a Six, Seven, Four, or Three, you "play on," because you allow him the chance of making a sequence; while, by playing a high card, you only leave him the chance of making a fifteen with a small one—that is, you "play off." Half the battle depends on whether you play "off" or "on;" but all must depend on your own judgment. Occasionally you may play on with a view to your own longer sequence; as for instance, he plays a Seven, and you hold a Five, Four, and Three. You play the Five in reply to his Seven, which allows him to play the Six, if he has one, and then you are able to come in with your Four, and perhaps win the Three to follow.

ODDS OF THE GAME.

The chances of points in a hand are calculated at more than four, and under five; and those to be gained in play are reckoned two to the dealer, and one to the adversary, making in all about six on the average, throughout the game; and the probability of those in the crib are estimated at five; so that each player ought to make sixteen in two deals, and onward in the same proportion to the end of the game; by which it appears that the first dealer has rather the advantage, supposing the cards to run equal, and the players likewise equally matched in skill. By attending to the above calculation, any player may judge whether he is at home or not, and thereby play his game accordingly, either by making a push when he is behind and holds good cards, or by endeavoring to balk the opponent when his hand proves indifferent.

IN FAVOR OF THE DEALER.

Each party being even 5 holes going up, is	6 to	4
at 10 holes each	12 ..	11
15 each	7 ..	4
20 each	6 ..	4
25 each	11 ..	10

Each party being at 30 each, is	9 to	5
35 each	7 ..	6
40 each	10 ..	9
45 each	12 ..	8
50 each	5 ..	2
55 each	21 ..	20
60 each	2 ..	1
When the dealer wants 3 and his opponent 4	5 ..	4
In all situations of the game, till within 15 of the end, when the dealer is 5 points ahead	3 ..	1
But when within 15 of the end	8 ..	1
And if the dealer wants 6, and the adversary 11	10 ..	1
Should the dealer be 10 ahead, it is .... 4 or	5 ..	1
And near the end of the game .... 10 or	12 ..	1
When the dealer wants 16, and the antagonist .... 11 ..	21 ..	20

AGAINST THE DEALER.

Both players being even at 56 holes each, is	7 ..	5
57	7 ..	4
58	3 ..	2
If the dealer wants 20, and his opponent 17	5 ..	4
When the dealer is 5 points behind, previous to turning the top of the board	6 ..	5
When he is 31, and the antagonist 36	6 ..	4
When 36, and the adversary 41	7 ..	4

EVEN BETTING.

When at 59 holes each player.
In all points of the game, till within twenty of the end, if the non dealer is three ahead.
The dealer wanting 14, and his antagonist 9.
Ditto............ 11, Ditto............ 7.

SIX-CARD CRIBBAGE.

This game is also played with the whole pack; it is the game most popular in this country; but both in skill and scientific arrangement it is vastly inferior to that played with five cards. Still, it is a pleasant resource in a dull hour, and abounds with amusing points and combinations, without taxing the mind much. It is played on the same board, and according to the principal portion of the rules of the preceding game. Its leading peculiarities may be thus summed up.

The dealer gives six cards to himself and his adversary. Each player lays out two of these for crib, retaining four in his hand. The deal and the "start" card is the same as at the five-card game, in like manner the pairs, sequences, fifteens, &c., operate, and the game point is sixty-one. The non-dealer, however, is not allowed any points at the beginning. The main difference between the games is, that in the game already described, the object is to get thirty-one, and then abandon the remaining cards; at the six-card game the whole are played out. There are more points made in the play, while, at five cards, the game is often decided by the loss or gain of one point. At Six-card Cribbage, the last card played scores a point. This done, the hands and crib are scored as at the five-card game; then another deal is played, and the victory is gained by the party who first gets sixty-one.

As all the cards must be played out, should one party have exhausted his hand, and his adversary have yet two cards, the latter are to be played, and, should they yield any advantage, it must be taken. For instance, C. has played out his four cards, and D. having two left (an Eight and Seven), calls fifteen as he throws them down, and marks three points—two for the fifteen, and one for the last card. Again, should D.'s two cards have been a pair (Threes, for instance), he marks two for the pair, and a third point for the last card. Speculating on this and other probabilities, you will always endeavor, when you are last player, to retain as close cards as possible, for this will frequently enable you to make three or four points, by playing your last two cards, when you would otherwise make but a single point. But this demands further illustration, as it is of paramount importance. For example:

Suppose you hold for the last two cards a Seven and Eight, and that your adversary has only one card remaining in his hand, the probable chance of its being either a Six or a Nine (in either of which cases you come in for four points) is eleven to two; therefore, it is only eleven to two but you gain three points by this play, exclusive of the end-hole; whereas, were you to retain, as your last two cards, a Seven, with a Ten, or any two cards similarly wide apart, you have no chance to score more for them than the end-hole, as there is no probability of their coming in for any sequence; or, if you can retain a pair of any kind for the last two cards (your adversary having only one card, and he being the first player), you by this means make a certainty of two points, exclusive of the end-hole. By the same rule you ought always to retain such cards as will (supposing your adversary to have none left) make a pair, fifteen, &c., for by this means you gain many points which you otherwise could not possibly get.

The calculations for throwing out at the five-card game are, for the most part, applicable to this. Still, there is not quite so much temptation to sacrifice the hand for the sake of the crib, as they do not both contain a similar number of cards. At this game the hand scores more than the crib, as there is one player always on the lookout to balk crib, while so many points being open to the play, offers a greater inducement to keep together a good hand. As soon as thirty-one, or the number nearest to it, be made in playing the hand, the cards should be turned down, that no confusion may come of their being mixed with the succeeding cards.

As before explained, in speaking of Five-Card Cribbage, your mode of conduct must be governed uniformly by the state of your game. Play to your score, and put the final result partially out of view. Whether it is your policy to play "on" or "off," must be ever the question in making up your judgment.

On an average, a hand, the moderns say, ought to yield about seven, and a crib five points. It is useful to remember this in laying out, and to note the difference between the odds of seven to five in favor of the hand here, and the superiority of the crib to the hand at Five-Card Cribbage.

The average number of points to be made each time by play is from four to five. The dealer has the advantage here, because he plays last. Pasquin considered that you were only entitled to twenty-five points for three shows and play, and that the dealer is at home if, when he makes his second deal, he is twenty-five points up the board, and when he deals for the third time, within eleven holes of game. The present system of calculation is to allow twenty-nine instead of twenty-five holes for the three shows, and to consider that at the end of the second round each player is at home at twenty-nine holes.

As you are on a parity at starting, being both at home, you will play with moderate caution your first hand, making fair risks, but not running into too wide speculations. On taking up your second hand, you will adapt your play to the relative scores on the board, as you have been told in relation to the other variety of the game, and will play "on" or "off," according to the dictates of policy. The same rule will govern your conduct during the remainder of the game; and should your adversary have gained the preference, or should you be more than home, both cases must be taken into consideration in playing your hand. If your cards present a flattering prospect, and you are by no means home, it is your duty to make a push, in order to regain the lead by running; whereas, should your adversary be better planted than you, and should you take up bad cards, it will be the best play to keep off, and only endeavor to stop your antagonist as much as possible, and thereby have a probable chance of winning the game, through his not being able to make good his points.

As so many points are to be gained in play by the formation of long sequences, you will frequently find it advantageous, having eligible cards for the purpose in view, to lead or play so as to tempt your adversary to form a short sequence, in order that you may come in for a longer. And this opportunity is particularly to be sought for, when a few holes are essential to your game, though gained at any risk. If you hold, as leader, a One, Two, Three, and Four, the best card to lead is the Four, since if paired, you answer with the Ace, and your adversary's second card may not form a fifteen.

THREE-HANDED CRIBBAGE.

The game of Three-handed Cribbage is not often practised. It is played, as its name imports, by three persons; the board being of a triangular shape, to contain three sets of holes of sixty each, with the sixty-first or game hole. Each of the three players is furnished separately with pegs, and scores his game in the usual manner.

Three-handed Cribbage is subject to the same laws as the other species of the game. The calculations as to discarding and playing are very similar; but it must be remembered that as all three are independent, and fight for themselves alone, you have two antagonists instead of one.

Five cards compose the deal. They are delivered separately,

and after dealing the fifteenth, another, or sixteenth card, is dealt from the pack, to constitute the foundation of the crib. To this each of the three players adds one card, and the crib, therefore, consists of four cards, while each individual remains with four cards in hand. The deal and crib are originally cut for, and afterwards pass alternately.

It is obvious that you will be still even, if you gain only one game out of three, since the winner receives a double stake, which is furnished by the two losers to him who first attains the sixty-first hole. It has been computed that he who has the second deal has rather the best chance of victory; but there seems very little difference.

Occasionally, at this game, some amusement arises from the complicated sequences formed in play; but ordinarily it is a poor enough affair. It will frequently happen that one of the three players runs ahead of the two others so fast, that it becomes their interest to form a temporary league of union against him. In this case they will strive all they can to favor each other, and regain the lost ground; and, in general, players will do well not to lose sight of this principle, but to prefer favoring the more backward of the adversaries, to giving the chance of a single point to the other. Such leagues, however, are a good deal resembling those between higher authorities—in the making of which, each enters a mental caveat to break it the first moment it suits his convenience.

FOUR-HANDED CRIBBAGE.

The game of Four-handed Cribbage is played by four persons, in partnerships of two and two, as at Whist—each sitting opposite to his partner. Rubbers or single games are played indifferently. Sixty-one generally constitute the game; but it is not unusual to agree, in preference, to go twice round the board, making the number of game one hundred and twenty-one.

At the commencement of the sitting, it is decided which two of the four players shall have the management of the score, and the board is placed between them. The other two are not allowed to touch the board or pegs, though each may prompt his partner, and point out any omissions or irregularities he may discover in the computation. The laws which govern Five-Card Cribbage are equally applicable here, as to the mode of marking holes, de-

5*

ficiencies in the counting, the taking too many points, etc. He who marks has a troublesome task, arising from the constant vigilance requisite to be exercised, in order not to omit scoring points made by his partner; his own gains he seldom forgets to take. He who does not mark should acquire the habit of seeing that his partner marks the full number he requires. Partners may assist each other in counting their hands or cribs—their interests being so completely identified.

It is most usual to play rubbers, and to cut for partners every rubber. The two highest and two lowest play together. The Ace is always lowest. In some circles they consider all tenth cards equal in cutting for partners: in others they allow of preference, according to rank, as at Whist. This would, however, be only applicable to cutting for partners. Also, in some cases it is the practice for the deal to go to the two who cut the lowest cards for partnership; but in general, the deal is decided by a subsequent cut between the two parties who are to score; the Ace being the lowest card, and all tenth cards being equal. If it is decided not to change partners after a game or rubber, there must be a fresh cut still for the deal. Each may shuffle the cards in turn, according to the laws which regulate this operation at Whist.

The deal and crib pass alternately round the table as at Whist, from right to left. The usual laws of Cribbage regulate the act of dealing, as to exposing cards, and so forth; and no one is suffered to touch their hands until the deal is complete. Before dealing, the cards must be cut in the ordinary way by your right-hand antagonist.

The dealer delivers five cards to each, in the usual mode, from right to left, one card at a time. The remainder of the pack he places on his left hand. Each person then lays out one card for the crib, which is of course the property of the dealer. The left-hand adversary must discard first, and so round the table; the dealer laying out last. There is no advantage in this, but such is the custom It is hardly necessary to say that the crib always belongs to the dealer.

As there is but one card to be laid out from the five received by each player, there is seldom much difficulty in making up your choice. Fives are the best cards to give your own crib, and you will never, therefore, give them to your antagonists. Low cards are generally best for the crib, and Kings or Aces the worst. Aces sometimes tell to great advantage in the play at this game. When your partner has to deal, the crib being equally your own, as if you had it in your proper possession, must be favored in the same way. Before discarding, always consider with whom the deal stands.

When all have laid up for the Crib, the pack is cut for the start-card. This cut is made by your left-hand adversary's lifting the pack, when you, as dealer, take off the top-card, as at Five-Card Cribbage. Observe that it is the left hand adversary who cuts this time, whereas, in cutting the cards to you at the commencement of the deal, it is your right-hand adversary who performs the operation.

Having thus cut the turn-up card, the player on the left-hand of the dealer leads off first, the player to his left following, and so on round the table, till the whole of the sixteen cards are played out according to the laws. Fifteens, sequences, pairs, &c., reckon in the usual way for those who obtain them. Should either player be unable to come in under thirty-one, he declares it to be a "go," and the right of play devolves on his left-hand neighbor. No small cards must be kept up, which would come in under a penalty. Thus, should A. play an Ace, making the number twenty-eight, and should each of the other three pass it without playing, not having cards low enough to come in,—on its coming round to A., he must play if he can under thirty-one, whether he gain any additional points by so doing or not. Example:

B. plays an Ace and makes thirty. Neither of the other three can come in, and on the turn to play coming round again to B., he plays another Ace and marks four points; two for the pair of Aces, and two for the thirty-one.

Many similar examples might be adduced, and there frequently arise difficult and complicated cases of sequences made this way out of low cards. Indeed, the playing out of the hand requires constant watchfulness on all sides; much more so than in Six-Card Cribbage. So many points are made by play in Four-handed Cribbage, that it is essential to play as much as possible to the points, or stages, of the game; sufficient data respecting which will be presently given.

In leading off, great care is necessary; not only at first starting, but after every "rest," or thirty-one. A Five is a bad lead, because the chances of a Ten succeeding it are so numerous; and an Ace is seldom a good lead, since, should the second player pitch what is highly probable, a tenth card, your partner cannot pair him without making the ominous number of twenty-one; a number equally bad at every description of Cribbage, since the next player has thus so good a chance of converting it, by another tenth card, into thirty-one. A Nine, again, is a bad lead, for should your left-hand adversary make fifteen with a Six, he cannot be paired by your partner, without making twenty-one. Bear this constantly in mind, and when possible to avoid it by equally good play, never either make the number twenty-one yourself, nor lead so as to compel your partner to do so. Threes or Fours form safe leads.

The second player will observe caution in pairing a card, so as not to give away the chance of six for a paltry couple, unless particularly wanting; or from some collateral reasons, he may consider it a safe pair; as in the case of the turn-up's being a similar card,—his holding the third of the same in his hand—the having seen one of the same already dropped, and so on. The same care must be shown in not playing closely on, unless compelled by the cards. Suppose your right-hand adversary leads a Three, it is obvious that if you reply with a Two or Four, you give your left-hand antagonist a good chance of forming a sequence, which he could not do had you played off. On the other hand, there frequently arise cases in which you feel justified in playing "on," purposely to tempt your adversary to form the sequence; in order to give your partner the chance of coming in for a still longer sequence. In many situations, a few holes may be of paramount value, gained at any risk. If the second player can make fifteen, it is generally better play than pairing the card led. Towards the end of the game it is sometimes important to retain cards all wide apart, when the object is merely to prevent your antagonist from making points in play; but as you only lay out one card, you have little chance of assorting your hand as you could wish.

The third player should aim at making the number below twenty-one, in order to give his partner a good chance of gaining the end-hole for the "go," or the two for thirty-one.

The dealer knowing he will have to play last the first round, will sometimes find it advantageous to hold Aces, or low cards for the purpose; particularly when it is essential to score a few holes in play, or when the only chance of game arises from the possibility of playing out. Holding Aces, it is frequently better play, when you have the option, to make twenty-seven or twenty-eight, than thirty, in order to have a chance of bringing in your Aces, which sometimes yield a heavy amount of points at that stage of the computation. When it is certain that the game will be decided in the course of the playing out of the hand, without coming to your show, you will keep good cards for playing at all hazards.

When the hand is played out, the different amounts are pegged, the crib being taken last. He who led off must score first, and so on round to the dealer. Each calls the number to which he considers himself entitled, and watches to see that they are scored properly; while at the same time he does not fail to scan his adversaries' cards with an observant eye, to see that, *through mistake*, they do not take more than their due.

The amount of points to be expected, on an average, from each hand, is seven, and from the crib about four to five. From the play, it is computed that each of the four players should make five points every time. Reasoning on these data, the non-dealers are at home, at the close of the first round, should they have obtained nineteen or twenty points, and the dealers are at home at the end of the first round, should they have acquired twenty-three or twenty-four. At the finish of the second round, with their average number, each set of players would be forty-two to forty-three. At the close of the third round, the non-dealers should be just out, or else the dealers will win. You must not, however, suppose there is any advantage to be gained from not having originally the deal; the chances are so various that the parties start fully equal; no matter whether with, or without the deal. From the above calculation, the game, going only once round the board, should be over in three rounds, both parties having a crib inclusive. Those who have not the first deal, have the original chance of winning, *if they can keep it*, by holding average cards throughout the game. Should they fail in making this good, the dealers (those who dealt originally are here signified,) will generally sweep all, having their second crib, and first show afterwards. As we have before intimated, it is quite as likely that the non-dealers will fail in holding "their own," as not. The non-dealers should observe moderate caution in the first hand, but under this head it is needless to say more to either party, than to impress it upon them again and again, to become thoroughly acquainted with the number of points which form medium hands, as well as the different stages of the game, and play accordingly. Moderate attention is all that is required to play Four-handed Cribbage well. It is a pleasant lively game, and when well conducted yields considerable amusement.

EXAMPLES OF HANDS.

We now give a few of the hands most common, and which the player will discover at a glance, without counting his cards before him.

Any sequence of three cards and a fifteen	count	5
Any sequence of four cards and a fifteen (as seven, eight, nine, and ten)	"	6
Any sequence of six cards	"	6
Any flush of four cards and a fifteen	"	6
Any flush of four cards and a pair	"	6
Two Aces, two twos, and a nine	"	6
A seven, eight, nine, ten, and Knave	"	7
Three twos and a nine	"	8
Two sixes and two threes	"	8
Two threes and two nines	"	8
Two sixes, a three, and a nine	"	8
A six, seven, eight, and nine	"	8
A six, five, and two sevens	"	8
Any double sequence of three cards and a pair (as Knave, Queen, and two Kings)	"	8
Any sequence of four cards and a flush	"	8
A six, seven, eight, nine, and ten	"	9
Two tenth cards (not a pair) and two fives	"	10
Two nines, a seven, and an eight	"	10
Two sixes, a seven, and an eight	"	10
Three fours and a seven	"	12
Three sixes and a nine	"	12
Three sevens and an eight	"	12
Three eights and a seven	"	12
Three nines and a six	"	12
Three threes and a nine	"	12
Three sixes and a three	"	12
Three sevens and an Ace	"	12
Two tens (pair) and two fives	"	12
Two nines and two sixes	"	12
Two eights and two sevens	"	12

EXAMPLES OF HANDS.

Two fives, a four, and a six . . . . . . count 12
Two fours, a five, and a six . . . . . . " 12
Two sixes, a four, and a five . . . . . . " 12
Two eights, a seven, and a nine . . . . . " 12
Two sevens, an eight, and a nine . . . . . " 12
Three fives and a tenth card . . . . . " 14
Four, five, and six of Clubs, and a five of Hearts turned up—(six for the sequences, three for the flush, four for the fifteens, and two for the pair of fives) . . . " 15
Two nines, a six, seven, and eight . . . . " 16
Two threes, two twos, and an Ace . . . . " 16
Any double sequence of five cards, as 1, 1, 2, 2, 3 . . " 16
Two eights, a seven, and two nines . . . . " 20
Two sevens, two eights, and a nine . . . . " 24
Two sixes, two fives, and a four . . . . . " 24
Two sixes, two fours, and a five . . . . . " 24
Two fives, two fours, and a six . . . . . " 24

Suppose you have a crib composed of
A five of Clubs,
Five of Spades,
Five of Diamonds,
And knave of Hearts,
With the five of Hearts turned up.
How many points would it count? Twenty-nine. Thus:—

Knave and five of Spades—fifteen 2
Knave and five of Diamonds—fifteen 2
Knave and five of Clubs—fifteen 2
Knave and five of Hearts—fifteen 2
Five of Spades, five of Diamonds, and five of Clubs—fifteen . 2
Five of Spades, five of Diamonds, and five of Hearts—fifteen . 2
Five of Spades, five of Hearts, and five of Clubs—fifteen . 2
Five of Diamonds, five of Hearts, and five of Clubs—fifteen . 2
Double pair-royal of fives 12
One point for the knave, being of the same suit as the card turned up 1

Total, 29

Many other hands might be given, but these are sufficient; the experienced player sees immediately he takes his cards in hand what they will make with the turn-up added.

Remember always that it is better to spoil your hand than to make your opponent's crib. Look well to the state of his game, and be not too ready in making holes in play. Be careful, watchful, and steady; and above all, *keep your temper!*

BÉZIQUE.

THIS interesting game is supposed to have originated in Sweden. It is said that during the reign of the first Charles—a reward having been offered by that monarch for the best game of cards, to combine certain requirements—a poor schoolmaster, by name Gustave Flaker, presented for the prize the game of cards which he called Flakernuhle, which was accepted by his royal master, and he made the happy recipient of the promised purse of gold. The game became very popular in Sweden, and was finally introduced into Germany, changed in some respects, and called Penuchle. There it also acquired great popularity.

It is only a few years since it was first introduced in Paris; but it has now become a favorite game with all classes there. It is played in the cafes, in the family circles, in saloons, and in fashionable assemblies. The French gave it the name of Bézique. Bézique is a variation of the game of *Cinq-Cents*, which has been played a long time in the provinces of the south of France. It has also borrowed somewhat from the game of *Mariage*, also an ancient game.

Bézique is fast becoming popular in the United States, and is now much played here in fashionable circles. It is known among our German brethren as *Peanukle*.

TECHNICAL TERMS USED IN BÉZIQUE.

BÉZIQUE (SINGLE).—The Queen of Spades and Knave of Diamonds.

BÉZIQUE (DOUBLE).—Two Queens of Spades, and two Knaves of Diamonds.

BRISQUES.—The Aces and Tens in the tricks *taken*.

COMMON MARRIAGE.—The King and Queen of the same suit, other than trumps.

ELDEST HAND.—The player immediately at the left of the dealer.

FOURS of Aces, Kings, Queens, or Knaves.

PACK.—The same as the Euchre, Piquet, or Ecarté pack, composed of thirty-two cards, all under the Seven spots being discarded.

QUINT-MAJOR.—Same as Sequence.

ROYAL MARRIAGE.—The King and Queen of trumps.

SEQUENCE.—Ace, King, Queen, Knave, and Ten of trumps.

STOCK.—The number of packs of cards corresponding with the number of players, shuffled together, and ready to be dealt.

TALON.—The cards remaining after the dealer has distributed eight to each player.

RULES OF THE GAME.

Bézique, as it is now played, has undergone great modifications since it has taken rank among the games in vogue. The manner of playing the game, the various modifications and counts, and the laws generally adopted, are here given.

1. Bézique is ordinarily played by two persons, with two or three packs of thirty-two cards (Euchre packs).

2. After having decided by lot, by turning two cards, which player deals, the one who deals hands the cards to be cut, and then distributes them by giving two cards, or three and two, till eight are dealt to each player, which is the number of cards almost always used in playing.

3. It is occasionally agreed to play with nine, and sometimes ten cards.

4. The number of cards having been decided and dealt to each of the players, the next card is turned up; this is the trump, which is the seventeenth if eight cards are played with, or the nineteenth if nine, or the twenty-first if it is with ten cards; that is, when two are playing.

5. After the dealer has placed the rest of the cards to his left (in this country we place the talon on the right), which forms the talon, his adversary plays first; and the one who wins the trick takes a

card from the talon in order to complete his number of eight, nine, or ten cards. The one who has lost the trick then takes a card in the same manner, and the play continues till the talon is exhausted. The winner of the trick has the privilege of the lead.

6. The following is the value of the cards, in making the tricks: 1st, the Ace, which takes all other cards; 2d, the Ten; 3d, the King; 4th, the Queen; 5th, the Knave; 6th, the Nine; 7th, the Eight; 8th, the Seven.

7. Before commencing the play, it is usual to decide on the number of points which is to make the game—that is, 1,000, 1,500, 2,000, or more.

8. When the turned-up card is not a Seven, the player holding the Seven of trumps can exchange it for the turned-up card—in which case he scores ten points.

9. The value of the combinations, in counting the points, are as follows:

Each Ace or Ten taken or saved in trick......counts 10 points.
Each Seven of trumps, when played or turned up " 10 "
The last trick............................... " 10 "
A common marriage.......................... " 20 "
A royal marriage............................. " 40 "
A Bézique.................................... " 40 "
Four Knaves................................. " 40 "
Four Queens................................. " 60 "
Four Kings.................................. " 80 "
Four Aces .... " 100 "
A sequence (*quint-major*).................. " 250 "
A double Bézique............................ " 500 "

10. It is permitted to decline following suit as long as there are any cards left in the talon; but the privilege ceases when the talon is exhausted; and, moreover, the player must, if he can, win the trick.

11. In a case of a misdeal, the hand passes, or you commence anew, according as your adversary may choose.

12. The player taking the trick *just previous* to exhausting the talon, may *then* declare any combination in his hand. The winner of the trick then takes the last card in the talon, and his adversary the trump card, and afterwards no combination can be declared or counted. The declared cards on the table must be taken in the

hand of each player, and the *rule imperatively is*, follow suit with the *highest in your hand*, and if you cannot follow suit, trump the trick.

13. The last trick having been made, each player counts the Aces and Tens which are in the tricks he has taken ; these Aces and Tens are called brisques. For each brisque the holder scores ten points, which are added to the score made during the playing by the combinations.

14. Brisques are not counted when any one of the players makes the game by scorings made by combinations ; that is to say, when neither of the players has made the number of points fixed to complete the game, then he who, with the brisques, counts most over the fixed number, wins ; and, in case of a tie, the winner is the one taking the last trick.

15. After all the cards have been taken in hand, if any player revoke by not playing the *highest in suit*, or refuse to trump when he has not suit in hand, his adversary may claim a deduction of forty points from the score of the player so revoking, or refusing to trump.

16. There are cases where one card is made to count several times. For example : a King which has counted in a marriage can count also in the score of 80 points (four Kings); it counts also in a score of 250. It is to be understood, in the last case, that it must be a King of trumps.

17. An Ace of trumps, which has counted in a score of 100 (four Aces), can also serve to make a score of 250 (sequence). The Queen of Spades and Knave of Diamonds, after having counted for a Bézique, can serve to count in a score of 250 (sequence), and the Queen of Spades in a marriage.

[We play differently in this country. The following is the rule here:—King and Queen of trumps, or any other suit once married, cannot again be married in the same hand, but may constitute one of four Kings or Queens, a sequence of trumps, or a Bézique, double or single. In other words, any card, *except either of those which have* been used to form Bézique, may serve to compose any other combination in which it has not previously been employed.]—*See note to Rule* 25.

18. If, after having scored an 80 of Kings, the same combination is filled in the hand, it also counts ; but neither of the first four Kings can be used to complete the combination. It is necessary— this is to be distinctly understood—that it must be a new combination.

19. The above rule holds good for Aces, Queens, and Knaves.

20. It is the practice, in order to escape errors, to place on the

table, with the faces up, all cards which have been used to make the combinations after they have been declared; that is, a marriage, a 100 of Aces, an 80 of Kings, a 60 of Queens, a 40 of Knaves, a Bézique, a 250, or a 500; but the player is privileged to play these cards when he pleases.

21. The possessor of a Bézique, sequence, or any other combination of cards in hand, must take a trick before declaring the same.

22. If a player declares Bézique, and subsequently is fortunate enough to draw cards sufficient to declare double Bézique, the latter counts 500 points, in addition to the 40 points already scored for Bézique.

23. When a single Bézique is in hand, it may be declared and placed upon the table, and there remain until the double Bézique is subsequently acquired. The player must judge from the condition of his hand whether it would be-better to try and achieve double Bézique, or abandon the effort for other combinations.

24. When a card is led, and other cards identical in value are played in the same round, the first card played takes precedence of *all* others of the *same denomination*, and wins the trick, unless it is trumped, or outranked by a card of superior value.

25. Only one combination may be declared at a time.

[In some coteries they play differently, and the fortunate holder of more than one combination may declare *all* such combinations upon taking a trick; but after Bézique has been declared, the cards composing *that* combination cannot be employed to form any *other*. It is, therefore, good policy to retain the Queen and Knave in hand, to aid in forming other arrangements of the cards, before declaring Bézique, particularly when Spades or Diamonds are trumps, for then the Queen may be serviceable in composing a royal marriage, sequence, or four Queens, while the Knave may avail in forming a sequence or four Knaves, and both may *afterwards* be employed to declare Bézique.]—*See Rule* 17.

26. Whenever a player neglect to take his card from the talon, he loses the play, or, left to the choice of his adversary, he can take the next two cards.

27. The play is equally void, at the choice of the adversary, when a player plays with a card too many; he must, if the play is not declared void, play twice in succession without drawing a card from the talon.

28. A player who, having only three cards, declares four and scores, must, when the error is discovered, correct the score by not counting it, and he can be compelled to play one of the three cards, if the error is not discovered before his adversary shall have played;

because this last would have been able, by reason of the error, to have thrown away a card which he supposed there was no reason to retain, since, on account of the error, he would not be able to count again by filling a combination.

HINTS AND CAUTIONS TO YOUNG PLAYERS.

1. It is presumed that a beginner is being instructed, and we say to him: You hold eight cards in your hand; you have led a card, and your adversary has taken it; you hold the Queen of Spades; your adversary having taken his card from the talon, you take yours; that card is the Knave of Diamonds; you have then a Bézique, but you say nothing; you wait till you take a trick, then declare it, and score 40 points; you have three Aces, and draw another from the talon; that makes a 100 of Aces, which you also declare when you take another trick—and so on, for as many combinations as you are fortunate enough to form in your hand. Whenever your adversary takes a trick, keep silent, wait patiently, for he is not allowed to score if he fails to make his declaration before you have taken the following trick.

2. It is good play to make your Aces and Tens whenever an occasion is presented for doing so, being careful, however, not to throw away the former when there is any likelihood of declaring four Aces. As the Aces and Tens count ten each in trick, the careful player, by a judicious use of small trumps and Aces of the suit led, may make an aggregate score at the end of the game of very respectable proportions. Remember, that *every* Ace or Ten you let your adversary take, scores twenty against you.

3. Do not fail to note, when your opponent displays a sufficient number of Bézique or sequence cards of the same denomination, to satisfy you that it will be impossible for you to form either of those combinations. This will enable you to improve your game by throwing away cards which might otherwise be retained with the false hope of making impossible combinations. For instance, we will suppose A. and B. to be playing at Bézique, with *one pack* of cards *each;* A. twice declares a common marriage in Spades, and also four Aces, two of which are trumps; it is therefore very evident that B. cannot make either a single or double Bézique, and it would be stupid in him to keep the Knave or Knaves of Diamonds in hand, unless in the anticipation of declaring four Knaves. Neither could B. hope

to make up the sequence, as A. had shown both trump Aces. It would therefore be policy in B. to play out the Tens and Knaves of trump in hand, whenever opportunity offered for doing so with profit. B. would thus relieve his play, and prepare for other combinations yet in the cards.

4. Be careful not to throw away in play either Bézique or sequence cards, while there is a reasonable probability of forming either. The reward for declaring those valuable combinations, particularly double Bézique, is so far beyond that of all others in the game, that it is good play to retain in hand any card which may serve to compose either of them, as long as *any chance* remains of achieving either.

5. If possible, avoid showing cards that will inform your antagonist that he cannot compose double Bézique or the sequence; you may thus embarrass and cramp his game, by preventing him from forming some more practicable combination, and frequently save Aces and Tens, which he would otherwise take from you.

6. It is preferable to retain the Kings and Queens in hand, until you can marry them. Therefore, when you are in a dilemma whether to throw away an Ace or a King, save the latter, when you can take the trick with the former. You will thus count ten, and in this way *may* count *all* your Aces in tricks; whereas, it is very difficult to declare four Aces and avoid losing some of them. It is true that four Aces count more than four Kings, but you have a reasonable hope of marrying the latter, and may then throw them into your opponent's tricks without injury to your own game. See *Hint* 2. It is possible thus to save all your Aces in trick, marry your Kings, and declare four Kings.

7. Do not forget to exchange your Seven of trumps for the card turned up, particularly if the latter is a sequence or Bézique card, and fail not to call for a score of ten for each Seven of trumps you play.

8. If possible, retain your Aces and Tens of trumps for the last eight tricks, and get the lead by taking the trick previous to exhausting the talon. You will thus compel your adversary to lose his Aces and Tens, by playing them on the cards you lead, and by being superior in trumps, you may take all the tricks, and make a very respectable score by this *ruse*. Besides getting the lead; you acquire the privilege of making the last declaration.

9. At the latter part of the game, just before the pack has "*gone from thy gaze,*" note what cards your antagonist has upon the table,

and make such use of this information as will "bring grist to your mill;" flank his Aces and Tens, and demoralize his hand generally.

BÉZIQUE WITHOUT A TRUMP.

This is played as the ordinary game, except that no card is turned to make a trump, but the trump is decided by the first marriage which is declared. For example: you or your adversary declare a marriage in Clubs, then Clubs become trumps, and so on with the other suits.

The quint-major of trumps, or the score of 250, cannot be declared until after the first marriage has been declared. The Seven of trumps in this game does not count ten points. The Béziques, four Kings, four Queens, &c., are counted the same as in Bézique when the trump is turned, and can be declared before the trump is determined. It is the same with the other cards which form combinations; their value remains the same as in the ordinary game of Bézique.

BÉZIQUE PANACHE.

In the game so called, the four Aces, four Kings, four Queens, four Knaves, must be, in order to count, composed of Spades, Diamonds, Hearts and Clubs; thus an 80 of Kings, composed of two Kings of Spades, one of Hearts, and one of Diamonds, does not form a combination; and in like manner with Queens and Knaves. This game ought to be the object of special agreement.

With respect to the combinations of the four points; the rules are those of ordinary Bézique.

BÉZIQUE LIMITED TO A FIXED POINT.

This game is played after an agreement made that the player who shall first have reached the point or number fixed for game, may stop on attaining the number of points agreed upon without playing the hand through. In this case, the player who claims to have won the game counts his points, adding to them his brisques; but if he is wrong (for example, when the game had been fixed at 1,500, and his points and his brisques only count 1,490, or less), the game is not continued, but is, on the contrary, gained by his adversary.

THREE-HANDED BÉZIQUE.

Bézique is sometimes played three-handed and four-handed. The following is the manner of playing three-handed Bézique: The game is begun, if two packs are played with, by throwing out one card, an Eight, no matter what color. After cutting for deal, the dealer has the cards cut by the player on his left, and distributes the cards by two or by three, commencing on his right.*

As in ordinary Bézique, and according to agreement, this game is played with eight, nine or ten cards.

The first to play is the player sitting to the right of the dealer, and, in like manner, the one to the right of the winner of a trick.

All the rules which apply to two-handed Bézique, in like manner, apply to this game.

FOUR-HANDED BÉZIQUE.

This game is usually played two against two, cutting for partners, and alternating every game; the players are also permitted to choose their partners, or may, in fact, play just as chance has placed them around the table.

The cards are cut and dealt as mentioned in the three-handed game.

In making a declaration and score, the rules are the same as in the ordinary game of Bézique.

The last trick counts ten points, or more if so agreed.

The partners unite their scores and their brisques, and count them as in the ordinary game of Bézique.

The laws governing the ordinary game are equally applicable to the four-handed game.

The partners should not be placed by the side of each other, but on opposite sides of the table.

---

*In this country, the dealer always deals the first card to his *left-hand* adversary, who, being the eldest hand, commences the round when the deal is completed, and the play continues throughout to the left; just the reverse of the French practice.

ALL-FOURS.

It is useless to inquire into the origin of this game; because, like many other games at cards, its birthplace and paternity are unknown. Its name, however, is derived from the characteristics of the game itself—the four chances or points consisting of *high*, the name given to the best trump; *low*, the designation of the smallest trump played in the round; *Jack*, the Knave of the trump suit; and *game*.

There are two distinct varieties of All-fours, in one of which the first card played by the non-dealer from his hand is the trump; and in the other, the trump is turned up from the pack. The last is generally known by the classic name of *Pitch*, or Blind All-fours. Certain terms are common to both games, the general characteristics being similar. All-fours is a very popular game in the South and Southwest, where it is known as "OLD SLEDGE," and "SEVEN-UP."

TERMS USED IN THE GAME.

High, the highest trump out; the holder scores one point.

Low, the lowest trump out; the original holder scores one point, even if it be taken by his adversary.

Jack, the Knave of trumps. The holder scores one point, unless it be won by his adversary, in which case the winner scores the point.

Game, the greatest number that, in the tricks gained, can be shown by either party; reckoning for—

    Each Ace *four* towards game.
    " King *three* " "
    " Queen *two* " "
    " Knave *one* " "
    " Ten *ten* " "

The other cards do not count towards game; thus it may happen that a deal may be played without either party having any to score for game, by reason of his holding neither court-cards nor Tens. In such a case, or in case of equal numbers—ties—the elder hand, the non-dealer, scores the point for game.

Begging is when the elder hand, disliking his cards, uses his privilege, and says, "I beg:" in which case the dealer must either suffer his adversary to score one point, saying "Take one," or give each three cards more from the pack, and then turn up the next card, the seventh, for trumps; if, however, the trump turned up be of the same suit as the first, the dealer must go on, giving each three cards more, and turning up the seventh, until a change of suit for trump takes place.

Eldest Hand.—This term is used in the four-handed game, and signifies the player immediately to the left of the dealer.

METHOD OF PLAYING ALL-FOURS.

The game is played with a full pack of fifty-two cards, which take rank as at Whist—the Ace being the highest and the Deuce the lowest. Any number of points may be played for; but it is common to state an uneven number, as five or seven; the last being most common.

The players cut for deal, the highest card having the deal, which is now the recognized law of the game. The Ace is highest—the other cards taking their regular order. Ties cut again. The dealer then gives six cards to each, three at a time, and turns up the thirteenth, if there be two players, and the twenty-fifth if there be four. The turn-up is the trump. The non-dealer then looks over his hand, and either holds it for play or begs, as already explained. If the Knave turn up, it belongs to the dealer, who scores one for it (but when the Knave is dealt to a player, and is taken in play by a higher card—Ace, King, or Queen of trumps—then the point is scored by the winner). The non-dealer having decided on his hand (it is not allowed to "beg" more that once, without it be previously agreed to do so), he plays a card of any suit. Then the dealer plays another card to this, and, if it be higher, he wins the trick, and plays another card, and so on throughout the six tricks. Each player must follow suit if he can, unless *he chooses to trump.* When the whole of the tricks are played out, the points are taken for high, low, Jack, game, as the case may be. Thus, one player may score a point for *high*, and the other for *low*; the greatest number, counting on the court-cards, Aces and Tens in each hand, reckoning for game. The winning the Knave, the making the Tens, and the taking your adversary's best cards, constitute the science of the game. The hand in which the Knave of trumps is eventually found, is the one which scores the point for the Jack. The *high* and the *low* always belong to the original possessor of those trumps.

LAWS OF ALL-FOURS.

1. A new deal can be demanded if, in dealing, an opponent's card is faced, or if the dealer in any way discover any of his adversary's cards; or if, to either party, too few or too many cards have been dealt. In either case it is optional with the players to have a new deal, provided no card has been played, but not afterwards.

2. If the dealer expose any of his own cards, the deal stands good.

3. No player can beg more than once in each hand, except by previous mutual agreement.

4. Each player must follow suit if he can, unless he chooses to trump, on penalty of his adversary scoring one point.

5. If either player score wrongly, the score must be taken down, and the adversary shall either score four points or one, as may have previously been agreed.

6. When a trump be played, it is allowable to ask the adversary if it be either high or low.

7. One card may count all fours; for example, the eldest hand holds the Knave, and stands his game; the dealer having neither trump, Ten, Ace, nor court-card, it will follow that the Knave will be both high, low, Jack, and game.

8. The points score in the following order · 1st *high*, 2d *low*, 3d *Jack*, and 4th *game*. Thus it will be seen that if two parties are playing, and the game stands six points each, he who scores high goes out first, as that takes precedence of the other points, unless Jack is *turned up* by the *dealer*. The same is the case when the game stands *five* to *six*: the former goes *out* on *high* and *low*, although the latter may make *Jack* and *game* in *play;* but if the former make *high, Jack*, the latter will go out on *low*.

9. Each Jack turned up by the dealer counts one point for him in the game, unless a misdeal occurs *before* the Jack is turned. If the dealer turns Jack and a misdeal occurs afterwards, even though it be in the same hand, or if he turns Jack and the cards run out by reason of the same suit being turned, he is not debarred from the privilege of scoring the point.

(*See " Decisions on Disputed Points,"* All-Fours, *notes II., VI., and X., pages* 149, 150. *and* 151.)

10. Should the same suit be turned until the cards run out, then the cards must be bunched, and dealt anew, but the last card must be turned for trump before a new deal can be claimed.

(See "*Decisions on Disputed Points,*" *All-Fours, note IV., page* 150.)

11. If a misdeal occurs, the dealer must bunch the cards and deal anew.

[The dealer deals again, otherwise he might make a misdeal puposely for the sake of getting the beg. The reason is embodied in the law maxim, that "a man cannot take advantage of his own wrong." A forfeits the deal, if B chooses to claim it, for his misdeal. But when the misdeal is to A's manifest advantage, A has to deal again, otherwise he would "take advantage of his own wrong." This decision also applies to the game of Pitch.]

THE FOUR-HANDED GAME.

All-fours is played by either two or four players; the same rules applying in this four-handed, equally as in the two-handed game.

The parties usually decide who shall be partners by *cutting* the *cards*, the two highest and the two lowest being partners. The four players divide themselves into two *sets*, each player sitting opposite his partner, as at *Whist*. The first deal is decided by *cutting* the cards, the lowest *cut* having the deal, but afterwards it is taken by each party alternately. When parties play for money it is usual to *cut for deal* at the commencement of each game. The *dealer* and the player on his *left only* are permitted to look at their cards previous to the latter deciding upon his hand, and in case he begs, the other parties must not raise their cards until the dealer announces whether he will "give one" or run the cards to another trump. This is done to prevent collusion between partners.

In some coteries privilege is granted to the dealer and eldest hand to *bunch the cards, i. e.*, to have a fresh deal provided they mutually agree to do so, after the latter has begged, and the cards have been *run* by the former; and sometimes, instead of *bunching* the cards, they mutually agree to run them, three more all around, and turn up a *new* trump. Again, it sometimes happens that a player will claim a new deal, because he has neither an Ace, face card, or trump in his hand. These modifications are played in some localities, but they do not belong to the regular game of ALL-FOURS, and, unless they have been agreed upon previous to commencing the game, they cannot be claimed as legitimate.

PITCH, OR BLIND ALL-FOURS.

This is played the same as the game just described, with the following exceptions:—1st. There is no begging. 2d. No trump is turned. 3d. The eldest hand has the privilege of making any suit he chooses trump, the first card he leads, or *pitches*, being trump. 4th. In the event of a tie in counting game no game is scored by either party.

[In the regular game of All-fours, in case of a tie, the non-dealer scores game to counterbalance the advantage the dealer possesses in having the chance of turning Jack. By parity of reasoning, some contend that the non-pitcher should score the game in case of a tie, to equalize the great advantage the pitcher has over his opponent in making the trump. We, however, incline to the opinion that it should not be scored to either party.]

In all other particulars, Pitch is played precisely the same as regular All-fours, and all the laws of the latter game apply to it with equal force, except the modifications enumerated and explained above. Pitch is by no means an uninteresting game, and in many localities has superseded the regular game of "Old Sledge."

(See "*Decisions on Disputed Points*," Pitch, *Rules V. and VII., page* 150.)

COMMERCIAL PITCH, OR, AUCTION ALL FOURS.

This is another game of "All-Fours," quite amusing and exciting in its character, especially as it may be played by as many as eight persons. It is subject to the usual rules of "All-Fours," and is played as here described:—

Before the game commences, it is usual to score ten points to each player, and each strives to wipe out this score, as in the game of Set Back Euchre. Every point a player makes is deducted from his score, and the first who wipes his score entirely out wins the game. The cards are shuffled, cut, and dealt as in the ordinary game, except that no trump is turned, and then commences the *commercial* part of the play, which is bidding for the privilege of making the trump. This is commenced by the eldest hand, who is said to "sell the trump." If, upon examination, the player next to the eldest hand thinks his hand is strong enough to make a trump, he bids, or declares how many points he will give the eldest hand to be allowed to make the trump—he may, for example, bid *two*—the next hand may bid *three*, while the third and fourth, not having good hands, decline to bid; and if no one is disposed to give more, the play begins by scoring the bid, which announces the pleasant fact, that the eldest hand has wiped out three points before a card has been played. Now, if the player who made the highest bid does not make the points bid, he loses, or is set back three points, so that he would have thirteen to make, while the eldest hand would have but seven to go. In this manner the game proceeds, each one retiring upon making ten points, until the players are reduced to two, and he who is finally beaten forfeits whatever may have been pending upon the issue of the game. If a pool has been made up to be played for, the first hand out wins. It sometimes happens when a player has four points scored, and thinks he can make four points, and the game, that he will bid four for the privilege of the pitch, but if he fails he is set back four points. If no player bids for the pitch, then the eldest hand takes that privilege, and pitches what trump he chooses. The player who makes the trump is compelled to pitch it. The trump must be put up for sale, but if the seller is offered less than he thinks he can make by pitching the trump himself, he may refuse to sell, and retain the privilege of the pitch; if, however, he fails to make the number of points he was offered for the pitch, then he is set back that number. There is another variety of the game, which differs from the above in the following particulars:—1st. The dealer sells the privilege of pitching. 2d. The player who buys the privilege of making the trump scores all the points he actually makes; but if he does not succeed in making all the points he bids, he is set back the number of points he falls short of completing his bid. For example: if he bids three, and only makes two points, he rubs out two points for those he has made, and is set back one point for that which he failed to make, and all the other players score for the point he come short of his bid. 3d. If none of the players bid for the trump, and it comes round to the dealer, then he (the dealer) pitches what trump he chooses, and scores for the point he makes. He is not, however, subject to any penalty, even if he does not make a point. The score of this game is kept the same as Bounce.

ALL-FIVES.

This game is played with an entire pack, in the same way as All-fours. But instead of nine or eleven, sixty-one points are played for, to constitute the game, which is marked on a cribbage-board. For Ace of trumps the holder marks *four* points when he plays it; for King of trumps, *three*; for Queen, *two*; for Knave, *one*; for the five of trumps, *five*; and for the Ten of trumps, *ten*. If the Knave, Ten, or Five be taken in play by superior cards, the points belonging to them are scored by the winner. In counting for game, the five of trumps is reckoned as five, and all the other Aces, Kings, Queens, Knaves, and Tens, are counted as in All-fours. A good deal of skill is necessary in order to play this game well: the proficient holding back a superior card to catch the Ten or Five. Trump after trick is not compulsory unless previously agreed to. The first card played by the non-dealer is the trump. The rest of the rules are the same as in All-fours. It may be played by four persons, either as partners or singly, and is a good merry sort of game.

FRENCH FOURS,

Sometimes called "*French Loo*," is a variety of All-Fours. It is played with a pack of fifty-two cards: three cards are dealt to each player, and the pack is turned with the cards exposed, face upwards, the top card being trump. Whoever *makes* or *takes* low, Jack, or game, scores a point for each. High is of course scored by the fortunate player who has it dealt to him, or draws it from the pack. There is no "begging" in this game, but the eldest hand, *i. e.*, the player next on the left of the dealer, may lead any card he chooses, and his opponent must follow suit. After each trick the dealer distributes one card, face up, to each player, beginning with the winner of the trick. Thus each player will have three cards in hand until the pack is exhausted. The game is otherwise governed by the same laws as All-fours. Two, four, or eight may play this game with a complete pack, but when any other number engage at it, sufficient unimportant cards must be taken from the pack before dealing, to make the deal go round without remainder. Thus—when three play, one card (usually the trey of one of the suits) must be rejected. The rejected cards must be exposed to the view of all the players. French Fours may be played with partners the same as the regular game of All-fours.

Apparently this game is more simple than All-fours, but such is not the case, for although each player may see what cards his adversary draws, yet where four play the game, a better memory and closer attention are essential than at the game of Whist.

CASSINO.

CASSINO is of Italian origin, and is a pleasant, simple game, when the stakes played for are not too high. It has the advantage of being a game that may be played by two, three, or four persons. But to understand the method of playing, it is necessary to recollect the

TERMS USED IN THE GAME.

Great Cassino, the Ten of Diamonds, two points.

Little Cassino, the Two of Spades, reckons for one point.

The Cards—when you have a greater share than your adversary, three points.

The Spades—when you have the majority of the suit, one point.

The Aces—each of which reckons for one point.

Lurched—when your adversary has won that game before you have gained six points.

The Sweep—matching all the cards on the board.

Building Up.—Suppose the dealer's four cards in hand to be a six, ten, and two aces—his adversary plays a six,—the dealer puts an ace upon it and says "seven," with a view of taking them with his seven—the non-dealer throws a deuce upon them and says "nine," hoping to take them with a nine then in his hand,—the dealer again puts upon the heap his other ace, and cries "ten," when, if his adversary has no ten, he plays some other card, and the dealer takes them all with his ten. This is called *building up*.*

THE MODE OF PLAYING CASSINO.

The following rules are given by Hoyle, and adopted by all his continuators:

* See Decisions on Disputed Points, folio 151.

THE MODE OF PLAYING CASSINO. 129

The dealer and partners are determined by cutting, as at Whist. The dealer gives four cards, one at a time, to each player; and either regularly, as he deals, or by one, two, three, or four at a time, lays four more, face upwards, upon the board, and, after the first cards are played, four others are to be dealt to each person, until the pack be concluded; but it is only in the first deal that any cards are to be turned up.

The deal is lost, if, in the first round, before any of the cards are turned up on the table a card is faced by the dealer; but if a card happen to be faced in the pack before any of the said four be turned up, then the deal must be begun again.

Each person plays one card at a time, with which he may not only take at once every card of the same denomination upon the table, but likewise all that will combine therewith; as, for instance, a Ten takes not only every Ten, but also Nine and Ace, Eight and Deuce, Seven and Three, Six and Four, or two Fives; and if he clear the board before the conclusion of the game, he scores a point. Whenever a player cannot pair or combine, he puts down a card.

The number of tricks must not be examined or counted before all the cards are played; nor may any trick but that last won be looked at, as every mistake must be challenged immediately.

After all the pack is dealt out, the player who obtains the last trick sweeps all the cards then remaining unmatched on the table.

In this game, the points gained by each party are counted at the end of each deal, and that party which has the least number of points scores nothing, but his points are deducted from the winning party's, who scores the difference towards game, which is eleven points.

A Tie precludes both parties from counting the points on which they tie. When three persons play, the two lowest add their points together, and subtract from the highest; but if their two numbers added together amount to or exceed that of the third player, then neither scores.

The principal objects are to remember what has been played; and when no pairs or combinations can be made, to clear the hand of court cards, which cannot be combined, and are only of service in pairing or in gaining the final sweep: but should no court cards be left, it is best to play any small ones, except Aces, as thereby combinations are often prevented.

In making pairs and combinations, a preference should generally be given to Spades, as obtaining a majority of them may save the game.

When three aces are out, take the first opportunity to play the fourth, as it then cannot pair; but when there is another Ace remaining, it is better even to play the little Cassino, that can only make one point, than to risk the Ace, which may be paired by the opponent, and make a difference of two points; and if great Cassino and an Ace be on the board, prefer the Ace, as it may be paired or combined, but great Cassino can only be paired.

Do not neglect sweeping the board when an opportunity offers; always prefer taking up the card laid down by the opponent, and as many as possible with one card; endeavor likewise to win the last cards or final sweep.

While great or little Cassino is in, avoid playing either a Ten or a Deuce.

When you hold a pair, lay down one of them, unless when there is a similar card on the table, and the fourth not yet out.

At the commencement of a game, combine all the cards possible, for that is more difficult than pairing; but when combinations cannot be made, do not omit to pair, and also carefully avoid losing opportunities of making tricks.

The points are thus calculated:

That party which obtains the great Cassino (or Ten of Diamonds) reckons................................	2 points.
Ditto, little Cassino (the Deuce of Spades)..........	1 "
The four Aces, one point each.....................	4 "
The majority in Spades...........................	1 "
The majority of cards............................	3 "
Besides a sweep before the end of the game, when any player can match all on the board, reckons........	1 "

STRAIGHT POKER.

SUCCESS in playing the game of Poker (or Bluff, as it is sometimes called) depends rather upon luck and energy than skill. It is emphatically a game of chance, and there are easier ways of cheating, or playing with marked cards, than in any other game. The game is played with a pack of fifty-two cards, and any number, from two to ten persons, form a party for Poker. In throwing round for deal, the lowest card gives the deal. Five cards are dealt out, one at a time, as in Whist. When a misdeal is made, the pool is doubled, and each player must put in an additional *ante*, and the eldest hand deals. This is called a "*double-header.*" It sometimes occurs that two misdeals are made in succession; in that case, each player must deposit another *ante* in the pool, and the deal again passes to the left. This is called a "*treble-header.*" No trump card is used, and after the first hand the winner of the "pool" always deals.

THE GAME.

An "*ante*" or stake is deposited in the centre of the table by the dealer; this is called the *Pool* or *Pot*. The dealer then throws round his cards singly, five to each player. The elder hand, or person on the left of the dealer, must then define his position. No cards are played out, as in ordinary games, but the player, after examining his hand, either says he will "*pass*" or bets a certain sum of money that he has the best hand, and puts up the amount of his bet into the pool. The next player must bet an equal sum on his hand, or else throw it up. And if the bets are not limited, he can bet or "*run over*" as much more as he pleases; and if he bets more, it is usual to say, "I see you, and go so much better," naming the amount "overrun;" the third player must fully cover the bet, or abandon his hand altogether; or he is allowed to bet still higher, if he wishes; and player number four must bet the same or go out. Thus the play goes round; and when it comes to the dealer's "*say*," if it so happens that the players have all made the same bets, he will also make the same bet if he pleases, and if he does he must "*call*" for a show of hands, and the game is then ended—the best hand taking the Pool. But should the dealer bet higher than the rest, or if any one of the party has increased the first bet before it reaches the dealer, the betting must still continue, and pass round, until the bets of all players are equal. The game cannot end until all the players have an equal stake in the Pool—the last person who bets to make the stakes all equal being obliged to "*call*" for a show of hands. Thus, if the bets go round a second time, should any one wish to bet still higher, it must pass round a third time, and so on. For example:—A., B., C., and D. are playing. D. is the dealer. A. leads, and bets one dime. B. puts down a dime. C. says, "I'll go a dime better," and he puts down two dimes. D., the dealer, must also put down two dimes; and he cannot end the game then, because he and C. have put two dimes in the Pool, while A. and B. have as yet only put in one dime. It now passes to A., who must put in another dime to make his bet equal, or throw up his hand altogether. It then passes to B. in the same way. Should they both put up the extra dime only, the game then ends with B., who must "*call*" for a show of hands—the highest one taking the Pool. But should either of these players go a dime (or any sum) better than C., the bet must go round past C. again, to give him an opportunity of raising his bet to the standard, and so on. When all the players "pass," and decline entering for the Pool, the chips are doubled, and each player must deposit another "*ante*" in the Pot; when this happens, the eldest hand deals. This is also a *double-header*. Where all the players refuse to equal a bet, the party making the bet takes the Pool without showing his cards. Should there be no limit or restriction to the betting, the player who has the most nerve, and bets the largest number of chips, usually takes the Pool; but it is a law imperative, that any player, if over-bet, may demand a "*sight*." Thus it sometimes happens, that a person with a poor hand will take the Pool, because he bets so high on his hand, that the rest think it is a good one, and are afraid to cover it. This is called "bluffing." Hence the game is sometimes denominated "Bluff." Hoyle so mentions it. In playing this game, the bets are generally limited to a certain amount. There is a variety of Poker where the deal passes round in succession, each player dealing in rotation. In playing this kind of Poker, a knife or key is passed around to show who has next deal, but in the above game the knife is passed to indicate who makes the next ante.

DRAW POKER

This game is played with a full pack of fifty-two cards, and any number of players from two to six may take part in it. It is governed by the same rules and penalties as Common Poker, and the same terms apply to it; indeed, it differs from that game in the following particulars only, viz.: In Draw Poker each player can discard from his own hand as many cards as he may choose, and call upon the dealer to give him the same number of cards from the pack, or he may throw up his whole hand, and call for a fresh one; but, before drawing the new cards, he must chip for the privilege of drawing, and hand those he discards to the dealer, or throw them in the centre of the table. The eldest hand discards first, and so in rotation round to the dealer, who discards last. The eldest hand, or indeed any of the other players, has the privilege of betting or "raising the pool" as high as he or they choose previous to drawing, provided there is no limit to the *ante*, and the other players must bet an equal sum, or abandon their chance for the pool. In Draw Poker the *Age* may pass, and cannot be debarred from the privilege of the last *say*. The *Age* does not use the term "I pass," as in Straight Poker, but merely says "*My Age*," which signifies he will wait for another *say*. The *deal* passes around in *rotation*, and the winner of the pool has not the privilege of a continued deal, as in Straight Poker.

TECHNICAL TERMS USED IN POKER.

Age.—(Same as Eldest Hand.)

Ante is the stake deposited in the pool by each player at the beginning of the game; lax players are frequently called upon to "*ante up*." Any bet in Poker is called an *ante*.

Blind.—The eldest hand has the privilege of making a bet before he raises his cards; this bet is usually limited to a few chips, and is called "going blind." The "blind" may be doubled by the player to the left of the eldest hand, and the next player to the left may at his option *straddle* this bet; and, if the dealer choose, he may, in turn double the *straddle*.

To illustrate this, we will suppose A, B, C, and D. to be playing a game of Poker: A is the dealer, B, who is eldest hand, goes a dime blind, and deposits that sum in the pool, C *doubles* the blind, and places two dimes in the pool, D *straddles* C, and puts four dimes in the pool, and A doubles the *straddle*, and deposits eight dimes in the pool. (In Straight or Draw Poker all this must be done previous to any of the parties seeing any of the cards dealt to them.) Now, if B, upon raising his cards, determines to *see* A, he must put fifteen dimes in addition to his original blind, C must go fourteen, D twelve dimes, and A eight dimes, which makes the sum of each equal. Any player, declining to *see* the blind, abandons his right to the pool. Eldest hand, *only*, has the privilege of starting the blind, but he may, if he chooses, delegate the right to another player. When the blind is not *doubled*, it may be *called* by depositing in the pool double the *ante* constituting the *blind*, and on coming round to the eldest hand he may "*make the blind good*" by depositing a sum making the blind equal in amount with the player who has *called it*, or abandon it, and "*pass his hand*." Any player has the privilege of *seeing* the blind, and running over it in his proper turn.

Bluffing off.—When a player with a weak hand bets so high that he makes his opponents believe he has a very strong hand, and they are deterred from "*seeing*" him, or "*going better.*" He thus gets the pool, and "*bluffs them off.*"

Brag.—Betting for the pool.

Call.—To call a show of hands, is for the player whose *say* is last to deposit in the pool the *same ante* bet by any preceding player, and demand that the hands be shown.

Chips.—Counters representing money, the value of which should be determined by the players at the beginning of the game.

Chipping, or to Chip, is synonymous with betting. Thus a player, instead of saying "I bet," may say "I chip" so much.

Double-Header.—When all the players "pass," and decline to enter for the pool, or where a misdeal occurs, the stakes must be *doubled*, and the dealer deals again.

Discard.—Taking one or more cards from your hand and placing them in the centre of the table, face downwards.

Draw.—To discard one or more cards, and receive a corresponding number from the dealer.

Eldest Hand, or Age.—The player immediately at the left of the dealer.

Filling.—To match, or strengthen the cards to which you draw.

Foul Hand.—A hand composed of more or less than five cards.

Going Better.—When *any* player makes a bet, it is the privilege of the *next player to the left* to *raise him*, or run over it, that is, to deposit in the pool the amount already bet by his adversary, and make a still higher bet. In such a case it is usual to say: "I see you, and go so much better," naming the extra sum bet.

Limit.—A condition made at the beginning of a game, as to the amount that may be bet on a hand. The limit of a game may be one dime, or the trifling sum of one thousand dollars.

Pass.—The privilege of declining to enter for the pool. The eldest hand first has this privilege, and so it passes in turn to the dealer. This is called *passing your hand.*

Raising a Bet.—The same as going better.

Say.—When it is the turn of any player to declare what he will do, whether he will *bet,* or *pass* his hand, it is said to be his *say.*

Seeing a Bet.—To bet as much as an adversary.

Sight.—Every player is entitled to a "sight for his pile," and when a player makes a bet, and his opponent bets higher, if the player who makes the first bet has not funds sufficient to cover the bet made by his adversary, he can put up *all* the funds he may have and *call* a show of hands for that amount.

Straddle.—See Blind.

Treble-Header.—When *all* the players have passed for two games in succession, or when two misdeals have been made in succession.

VALUE OF THE CARDS.

The cards count by Pairs, by Two Pairs, by Triplets, by Flush, by Full, and by Fours. Sometimes straights or sequences are counted.

ONE PAIR.—Two cards of the same denomination. For example: Two Deuces are the lowest, and two Aces the highest pairs. The pair may be of any color.

TWO PAIRS.—Two pairs of different cards in the same hand count next to a single pair. Aces and Kings are the highest, and Deuces and Treys are the lowest two pairs.

STRAIGHT SEQUENCE, or ROTATION, is five cards following in regular order of denomination, as Ace, Deuce, Trey, Four, and Five, and the cards may be of different suits; a Straight will beat two pairs. In some coteries a Straight Flush outranks four cards of the same denomination. In a Straight the ace plays both ways, but its value is different. When with the King, Queen, Knave and Ten, it makes the highest straight; when with Deuce, Trey, Four and Five, the lowest.

Straights are not considered in the game, although they are played in some localities, and it should always be determined whether they are to be admitted at the commencement of the game.

TRIPLETS are three cards of the same denomination, and rank

higher than two pairs. For example:—three Deuces beat a pair of Aces and Kings.

A FLUSH is five cards all of the same suit, and beats three Aces. Should it so happen that two Flushes are dealt in the same deal, the winning hand must be decided by the denomination of cards composing the Flush. Thus, a Flush, with an Ace highest, would beat a Flush with King highest.

FULL HAND is three cards of the same denomination, and a single pair. A Full ranks higher than a Flush; for example:—two Deuces and three Treys will beat a Flush.

FOUR of the same denomination is the highest combination of the cards in Poker, and four Deuces will beat a full hand of Aces and Kings. Therefore, the only certain winning cards are four Aces, or four Kings and an Ace. Should two or more hands come together of equal value, in pairs, the best of them is decided by the side cards. (*See Law* 32.)

[It is strongly urged by some experts that the strongest hand at Draw Poker should be a *Straight Flush*, for the reason that it is more difficult to get than four of a kind, and removes from the game the objectionable feature of a known invincible hand. It is *impossible* to tie four Aces or four Kings and an Ace, but it is *possible* for four Straight Flushes to be out in the same deal. No gentleman would care to bet on a "sure thing," and we therefore think the Straight Flush should be adopted when gentlemen play at this game.]

LAWS OF DRAW POKER.

1. The game of Draw Poker is played with a pack of fifty-two cards.
2. At the outset of the game, the deal is determined by throwing around one card to each player, and the player who gets the highest card, deals.
3. In throwing for the deal, the ace is highest and the deuce lowest. Ties are determined by cutting.
4. If a player lets a card fall in cutting, that is his cut; and, if he shows two, the highest is his cut. Less than three cards is not a cut.
5. After the first hand is played, the deal passes from right to left in regular succession, and each player takes the deal in turn.

[In Straight Poker, the winner of the pool deals.]

6. The cards must be shuffled above the table; each player has a right to shuffle the cards, the dealer last.

7. The player at the right of the dealer cuts the cards.

8. Five cards must be dealt to each player; one at a time, commencing with the player to the left of the dealer, and, if a card is faced in the pack, a new deal may be demanded.

9. If a card be accidentally exposed by the dealer while in the act of dealing, the player to whom such card is dealt *must* accept it as though it had not been exposed. (*See Law* 21.)

[This rule does not apply when a card is faced in the pack.]

10. If the dealer gives to himself or either of the other players *more* or *less* than five cards, and the player receiving such a number of cards discovers and announces the fact *before* he raises his hand, it is a misdeal, and the dealer must shuffle and deal the cards again.

11. If the dealer gives to himself or either of the other players more or less than five cards, and the player receiving such a number of cards *raises* his hand before he announces the fact, no misdeal occurs, and he must stand out of the game until the next hand. (*See* "*Decisions on Disputed Points,*" *I., II., III., and XI., pages* 141, 142, *and* 143.)

12. After the deal has been completed, each player may discard from his hand as many cards as he chooses, and call upon the dealer to give him a like number from those remaining in the pack, or he may throw up his whole hand and call for a fresh one.

13. Previous to receiving fresh cards from the pack, each player must place in the centre of the table the discarded ones, which cannot again be taken in hand under any circumstances.

[*Decision.*—A, B, C, and D are playing Draw Poker. D is dealer. They have all drawn and D lays off one card, and then takes up his hand and finds he has a full; he does not take the card, but bets for the pot with his contented hand. Has D the right to bet his hand as he did; or is he, because he laid that card off, obliged to take it? *Answer.*—The dealer must take the card he has laid off.]

14. Before discarding and drawing from the pack, each player must chip in the pot or pool for the privilege of drawing.

15. The eldest hand must discard first, and so in regular rotation round to the dealer, who discards last, and all the players must discard before any party is helped.

16. Any player may demand of the dealer how many cards he drew, and the latter must reply, any time before a bet is made. The first bet puts an end to the right to inquire, and removes the obligation to answer.

17. Previous to drawing from the pack, any player in his proper turn may bet or raise the pool as much as he chooses, provided there is no limit to the game, and his opponents must bet an equal sum, or more, unless they pass out and abandon their chance to win the pool. Should the game, however, have a limit, no player can bet more than the sum agreed upon as the limit at the commencement of the game.

18. A player cannot go *blind* after the cards are cut. Should the eldest hand go *blind*, the other players must see the blind before they draw to their hands, or else pass out of the game.

19. Should the dealer give any player *more* cards than the latter has demanded, and the player announces the fact before he raises the cards, the dealer must draw one of the cards and restore it to the pack. But if the player raise the cards before informing the dealer of the mistake, he must stand out of the game during that hand.

20. Should the dealer give any player fewer cards than the latter has discarded, and the player announces the fact previous to lifting the cards, the dealer must give the player from the pack sufficient cards to make the whole number correspond with the number originally demanded. If the player raises the cards before making the demand for more, he must stand out of the game during that hand.

21. If a player discards, and draws fresh cards to his hand, and while serving him the dealer exposes one or more of the cards, the dealer must place the exposed cards upon the bottom of the pack, and give to the player a corresponding number from the top of the pack. (*See Law* 9.)

[*Decision.*—A, B, C, and D play at the game of Draw Poker. A deals, and B chips and asks for three cards. While helping him, A accidentally turns up one of the three cards. Has B the privilege of electing whether to accept or decline the card thus exposed? *Answer*—B has no choice in the matter, and cannot receive the card. If this rule prevailed, B might accept the card if it was of the suit or denomination he desired, or decline it, if of no value in making his hand, and thus have two chances, which would be a manifest injustice to the other players.]

22. The eldest hand (*age*) has the privilege of passing once, and afterwards coming in the game again to brag. After the ceremony of the deal has been concluded, the player who is eldest hand says: "My age," which signifies he passes.

[No other player has this privilege at the game of Draw Poker, but the reverse of this rule applies when playing Straight Poker, and at that game *any* player may pass with the privilege of coming in again, *provided* no player preceding him has made a bet.]

23. Should the eldest hand, or age, and the other players chip to

fill their hands, and after all the hands are full should the players all pass, then the pool is forfeited to the eldest hand.

24. Should all the players pass without chipping to fill their hands, then the pool becomes a "double-header;" the ante is doubled, and the deal passes to the eldest hand.

25. Should any player in his regular turn brag or bet any sum within the limit of the game, his opponents must call him, go better, or pass out of the game.

26. Should a player call an opponent, both parties must show their hands, the caller last, and the best poker hand wins.

27. When a player brags, and his opponents decline to call him or go better, he wins the pool, and cannot be compelled to show the value of his hand.

28. When a player is called he must show all the cards in his hand, and any player who has bet for the pool, although he may subsequently have passed out, has a right to see what cards his opponent wins the pool upon. (*See "Decisions upon Disputed Points," Draw Poker, Note IX., page* 143.)

29. If a player passes, and afterwards discovers that he has a winning hand, he cannot come in the game again during that hand, but must relinquish all claim to the pool. (*See "Decisions upon Disputed Points," Draw Poker, Note XV., page* 144.)

30. None but the eldest hand (age) has the privilege of going a blind, but he can delegate this right to the next player. The party next and to the left of the eldest hand may double the blind, and the next player straddle it, the next double the straddle, and so on until the same reaches the dealer. (*See Terms used in Poker, page* 133.)

31. When a player makes a bet, and his opponent bets higher, if the player who makes the first bet has not funds sufficient to cover the bet made by his adversary, he can put up *all* the funds he may have and *call* a show of hands for that amount.

[If the player calling for a show of hands has the best one, he wins the ante, and an amount from each player who bets over him, equal to the sum that he himself has bet. The next best hand is entitled to the balance of the bets, after settling with the caller.]

32. If, upon a *call* for a show of hands, it occurs that two or more parties interested in the call hold hands identical in value, then the parties thus tied must divide the pool, share and share alike, provided, no party likewise interested should hold a hand superior in value. Where ties occur in pairs the best hand is decided by the value of the other cards.

WHISKEY POKER.

This is a neat variation of Draw Poker, and is a most amusing game. Each player contributes one chip to make a pool, and the same rules govern as at "draw," except that the strongest hand you can get is a straight flush. Five cards are dealt to each player, one at a time, and an extra hand is dealt on the table, which is called the "*widow.*" The eldest hand then examines his cards, and, if in his judgment his hand is sufficiently strong, he passes. The next player then has the privilege of the widow, and for the purpose of illustration we will suppose he takes it; he then lays his discarded hand (that which he relinquishes for the widow) face up in the centre of the table, and the next player to the left selects from it that card which suits him best in making up his hand, and so on all around the board, each player discarding one card, and picking up another, until some one is satisfied, which he signifies by knocking upon the table. When this occurs, all the players around to the satisfied party have the privilege of one more draw, when the hands are shown, and the strongest wins. If any player knocks before the widow is taken, the widow is then turned face up, and each player from him who knocks has but one more draw. Should no one take the widow, but all pass to the dealer, he then turns the widow, and all parties have the right to draw until some one is satisfied.

STUD POKER.

Is the not very euphonious name of a game which, in all essential particulars, is like the other Poker games, and is subject to the same laws, and mode of betting, passing, etc. It is played in this manner:

Five cards are dealt, one at a time—the first dealt, as usual, face down, all the others face up, the higher pair, or best hand, winning, as at "draw." To illustrate, suppose the dealer's four cards as exposed, are a King, four, seven, and a five; and his opponent's a Queen, ten, six, and nine—the dealer's hand in sight, is the better hand, but the call being made, and the unknown cards turned over, the non-dealer shows an ace, and his opponent an eight; of course the dealer loses

DECISIONS ON DISPUTED POINTS.

In games of all kinds, as well as in bets, questions often arise which the rules or laws designed to cover the case do not reach, or upon which there are different views as to the true interpretation of the laws. Indeed, it would be impossible to establish a code of laws for this purpose, that should meet with unerring certainty every conceivable contingency, just as it is impossible to do the same thing in political economy. Hence, when such questions arise, they must be submitted to what may be termed the unwritten common law or equity of games; and decided, as the lawyers say, "according to equity and good conscience."

To render "THE CARD PLAYER" complete in all its departments, we have compiled from "*Wilkes' Spirit of the Times,*" which is generally accepted as the ablest exponent of the laws of games, the solutions of a variety of "vexed questions," which embrace many points on which disputes or misunderstandings are most likely to arise. The decisions are founded, as will be readily admitted, upon the principles of common justice and equity, or what might perhaps be properly termed "the logic of games;" and will be accepted as putting at rest the disputed points to which they refer.

STRAIGHT AND DRAW POKER.

I. A, B, C, and D are playing a game of Straight Poker. A deals, B passes, C and D chip. A, the dealer, raises his hand and discovers he has dealt himself six cards. Is it a misdeal, and to be dealt over, or does A lose his hand? *Answer.*—The dealer loses his hand, but it is not a misdeal. The dealer should have discovered his hand was foul before he raised his cards.

II. A, B, C, and D are playing a game of Poker. A deals, B chips, C passes; D, holding a flush, runs over B; A passes; B sees D and runs over him; D calls him, and upon B showing his hand it is discovered that he has but four cards, which are, however, four aces. Can B claim the pool? *Answer.*—B cannot win the pool

Having only four cards, his hand is foul, and he might for that reason have called for a fresh deal. It is not equitable to allow a player to take the pool on a hand upon which he might claim a new deal, if it were for his advantage to do so.

III. In playing a game of Draw Poker, the dealer gives himself six cards, but upon raising his hand discovers the mistake, and announces it to the board before any party has drawn. Is he ruled out and the other players allowed to draw, or should there be another deal? *Answer.*—The dealer loses his hand. It is the business of the player to see that he has *five* cards, no more or no less, before he raises them. If he raises the hand and it proves foul, he must stand out of the game until the next deal. If he does not raise it, it is a misdeal.

IV. At a game of Draw Poker, the player next to the dealer asks for three cards, and has four served to him, but does not discover the fact until one or two others have been served by the dealer; still he does not raise the cards, and immediately informs the dealer of the mistake. What should be done in a case like this? *Answer.*—The dealer must draw one of the four cards, and restore it to the pack.

V. In a game of Draw Poker, suppose the eldest hand goes a blind, the next straddles the blind, &c.; must the dealer make the blind good before any cards are dealt; also, must all the other players do the same? *Answer.*—When there is a blind, the player must "see" the blind, not before the cards are dealt, but before they draw to their hands.

VI. A, B, C, and D are playing Draw Poker. D is dealer. They have all drawn and D lays off one card, and then takes up his hand and finds he has a full; he does not take the card, but bets for the pot with his contented hand. Has D the right to bet his hand as he did; or is he, because he laid that card off, obliged to take it? *Answer.*—The dealer must take the card he has laid off.

VII. A, B, C, and D are playing at Straight Poker, A being the dealer, and B having the age. B passes on his privilege; C also passes. D brags five chips; A also brags. B comes in upon his privilege; C also bets, but D demurs at his doing so, and contends that C, having passed upon his first say, passed out of the game, and cannot come in again to bet during the hand. Which is right? *Answer.*—C is right. If any player had bragged previous to C's passing, then he (C) would have been ruled out; but as no bet was made prior to his passing, he has the privilege of betting, just the same as if he had not passed. It is an established rule in Straight Poker, that a player may pass, and come in again to bet, provided no other player has previously bragged.

VIII. In playing Poker, when straights or routines are played, does ace play both ways? ace, deuce, tray, four and five, and ace, king, queen, jack, and ten? Or does ace, deuce, tray, four and five constitute a routine? *Answer.*—The ace plays both ways, but its value is different. When with the king, queen, knave and ten, it makes the highest straight; when with deuce, tray, four and five, the lowest.

IX. Has a player who *calls* another in a game of Poker a right to see the whole of his hand, or can the party so called show only a portion of his hand—(a pair, for instance), and demand that the caller beat that before showing more? *Answer.*—The party who is called must show his whole hand. Poker is a *show* game, and any party who *brags in a pool* must show his hand to the board, if required to do so, even if he relinquishes his chance of winning; because his adversaries have a right to know whether he is trying to bluff them, without a hand to support it. After a party once bets, any other player who also bets has a right to see what hand his opponent brags upon. If a player wins the pool without being called, his adversaries have a right to see his cards *back up;* otherwise he might brag or bet with six or more cards. But if any player throws his cards with the pack, he cannot call for a show. To do this he must retain his cards in his hand.

X. A deals B three cards (one each time, as in Poker), and himself three. B holds three aces, and A holds three diamonds (a flush); both parties agree to abide by the rules of Poker, or Bluff, and consider the three cards as representing a hand of said game. Which wins? *Answer.*—B wins. If three cards are to make a hand, three of a kind are a *full* hand, and beat a flush of three.

XI. A, B, C, and D are playing at Draw Poker; each one chips for the privilege of drawing cards. Can C bet five chips before he gets his cards, and oblige B to bet five chips, in order to get the cards he has already put up one chip to draw? Or, in other words, after a player has chipped and called for, say, three cards, can an opposing player chip higher and compel him to respond to this larger bet, or relinquish the privilege of drawing? *Answer.*—In the case stated, *i. e.*, before the cards are drawn, C can raise as much as he likes within the limits of the game, if there be one, and all the other players must put up chips equal to the raise, or abandon their hands. Thus—when C raises B's bet four chips, he (B) must put up four more before he can draw.

XII. A, B, C, and D play at the game of Draw Poker. A deals, and B chips and asks for three cards. While helping him, A accidentally turns up one of the three cards. Has B the privilege of electing whether to accept or decline the card thus exposed? *Answer.*—B has no choice in the matter, and cannot receive the card. If this rule prevailed, B might accept the card if it was of the suit or denomination he desired, or decline it if of no value in making his hand, and thus have two chances, which would be a manifest injustice to the other players. When an *original* hand is being dealt, then, if a card is exposed by the dealer, the party to whom it is dealt *must* take it.

XIII. A, B, C, and D play a game of Straight Poker. A deals, B goes blind, C looks at his cards and passes. D proposes to straddle the blind, which is objected to by B, on account of C's passing. Can his (B's) objection be sustained? *Answer.*—B is right; C having passed, prevents D's straddling the blind.

XIV. A, B, C, and D are playing Poker, with full blind—that is, if one goes blind, next straddles, it would cost the next man double the whole blind. A goes blind a quarter of a dollar. B straddles A's blind. C fills the blind. D lays his hand. A cannot fill. The question arises as to the amount it costs B to call C. *Answer.*—It costs C a dollar to see the blind, and therefore it will cost B half a dollar to fill.

XV. At a game of Poker, A "chips," B calls him and holds to A's view an ace (while the rest of the party are passing). A says, "You have not two of those? if so, they beat me." B replies yes, and the rest having passed out, shows them; they being acknowledged good, puts the hand to the deck. A running his hand over again, discovers two pairs in his, and says, "Hold on, I have better," and shows them. Can A claim the money under these circumstances? *Answer.*—A cannot. He must discover his good hand before he acknowledges B's to be good, and let it go to the pack.

XVI. A, B, and C are playing Poker. A deals the cards; B draws five cards, C draws one; B bets one check, C bets twenty-five checks; B puts up twenty-five checks, all that he has before him, and borrows fifteen dollars and bets C. C has $100 in checks; he puts them up, and then B calls out what he has, without C saying any thing. The point is, whether B can hold C responsible for the money under these circumstances? *Answer.*—He can only hold C for what he (B) has up.

XVII. Seven persons, A, B, C, D, E, F, and G, are engaged at Draw Poker. A deals, and the hands are all made. B passes to C, who bets, and after C thus bets, D demands from the dealer (A) to be told how many cards he (the dealer) drew. A demurs to reply, claiming that D should have used his eyes, as all was done openly, and without attempt at concealment. Is the dealer bound to answer D's question, or, if compelled to answer, must not the question be put at the time the dealer makes up his hand? *Answer.*— Any player may demand how many cards the dealer took, and the latter must reply, up to the time a bet is made. The first bet puts an end to the right to inquire, and removes the obligation to answer.

XVIII. A party of five are playing Draw Poker, N (dealer), L, M, G, and A. L is blind. M and G pass. A fills the blind. N (dealer) passes. L makes good the blind, and raises it five dollars, and A calls the raise. L draws three cards, and A also calls for three; but A, on discarding, discovers that two cards were stuck together, and, consequently, that he had six cards in his original hand. He immediately, and before seeing the cards he called for, announced the fact to the board, and L claims the pot, including the money A had put up. Is he entitled to it? *Answer.*—It is L's money. A's hand is foul.

XIX. A, B, C, and D are playing a game of Poker, with the age. A deals, B goes a blind, C straddles or doubles over B's blind. If all the parties come in (B and C each making their blind good), who has the age? *Answer.*—When all make good, the player next the dealer has the age.

XX. In playing Draw Poker, the eldest hand or *age* chips, and the other players also chip, to fill their hands. After all the hands are full, the age and other players pass. Can the age take the pot without chipping again for it, or is it a double-header? *Answer.*— The eldest in the case stated takes the pot. It only becomes a double-header when all *pass before* the hands are helped.

XXI. A, B, C, and D are playing the game of "poker;" the "ante" is twenty-five cents; each player, as he "antes," passing the "buck" to his left-hand adversary, as usual. Now, 1st. A "antes," passing the "buck" to B. Has B got the right to "ante" immediately, making the pool fifty cents, and pass "buck" to C, instead of waiting till the next deal? 2d. If he has that right, can it be invalidated by any one objecting to its being done? *Answer.*—He has not the right. He may go "blind" if he chooses, but he cannot get rid of the "buck."

XXII. A, B, C, and D play a game of Straight Poker. A deals, B goes blind, and all the four players simply make the blind good. The question is, whether, as no one has raised the blind, there can be any more betting, or whether the best hand takes the pool? *Answer.*—The highest hand takes it. When the man who went blind simply made it good, it was equivalent to a call. As he did not raise it, there could be no more betting.

EUCHRE.

I. How many points does a lone player lose if he fails to win three tricks? It is customary in some circles, and clubs even, for the opponents to count but two points only, when the person who plays alone against them does not win three tricks. This practice is quite extensively adopted in the New England States, where, however, the game is comparatively but recently introduced; and there, too, it is sometimes permitted to score *three* points under such circumstances; but by what analogy or authority does not appear. Various reasons are given for the practice, the principal one of which seems to be, that the risk of the lone player's opponents is not increased, but rather diminished, by the withdrawal of one opponent from the round, and therefore they ought not to count more than they could claim if their two opponents both played together against them; and moreover, that the lone player having to contend, single-handed, against his two adversaries, he ought not to be compelled to pay so heavy a penalty as four points for the defeat. In almost every other portion of the United States, however; in fact, everywhere now-a-days, where *Lap* and *Slam* are comprehended and played, the party playing alone, and failing to win three tricks, loses four points. Some few good old players, who ought to know better, object to the Lap, &c., and declare it not Euchre; and we remember—and are not the oldest inhabitant either—that the same kind of objection was urged, and in like manner, against the practice of playing alone—now fondly cherished as one of the most attractive events in play—when, about a quarter of a century ago, it was first explained to some players, to whom it was then a novelty, as part and parcel of the play!

In favor of counting four points for the euchre of a lone hand, it is claimed that if the risk of the two players is not increased by the withdrawal of one of their antagonists, yet the gain of the lone player is doubled if he wins all five tricks; and if he does have them both to contend with, single-handed, yet he encounters them voluntarily—challenges, defies them to the strife, with full knowledge of the consequences—availing himself of what he judges to be a highly favorable chance to win four points to his score. If successful he does score them, and surely there can be no valid reason why he should be permitted to gain twice the number of points he runs the risk of losing. Besides, such a practice bears no analogy with any principle of the game. Indeed, when all the players are in, and one side, at the score of four, if contending for the point only, are euchred, their opponents are allowed to score two, in this case really losing double as much as they aim to win. But those two points are allowed to the winning party, only because the other side, though playing but for one point, might possibly have made a march—thus equalizing the loss or gain to the risk. To allow four points for the euchre of a lone player is the universal rule here (Washington); and, indeed, skilful players everywhere, who thoroughly comprehend the mysteries and science of the game, approve and confirm the practice. Your sanction and judgment in the case will greatly oblige many lovers of this entertaining game.

Answer.—We are not to alter or make the law, but only to declare it. So far as we are concerned, the question is *res judicatæ*. Our correspondent argues shrewdly, but there is a good deal to be said on the other side. He says that now-a-days, wherever "Lap and Slam" are comprehended, the lone player who fails to take three tricks loses four. To this we reply that "Lap and Slam" are totally unknown in many places where *Euchre* is the game most in favor. We speak of the West. We have often played the game there, and have seen it played hundreds of times, but never heard of "Lap and Slam" among the players. It may be very good, but it is not Euchre, and our correspondent asks for the rules of Euchre. It seems clear enough to us why the two who play against a lone hand should score but two for a euchre. They only make a euchre—three tricks—while, to score four, the single player must get all five. If he takes three, he scores but one; if they take three, they score two. This is the established odds of the game. It might be reasonable to let them score four, if *they* take all the tricks, but this will never occur. Scoring four is an extraordinary privilege beyond the general order of the game, and the conditions of it are these: One player shall play his hand against both his opponents, and he shall take all five of the tricks.

II. 1. In playing the game of Euchre, when I assist my partner, can he play it alone? 2. My partner makes or takes up a trump, can I play it alone? 3. When an opponent takes up a trump, makes a trump, or orders me up, can I play alone against him? 4. If an opponent play it alone, can I play alone also? 5. If my partner pass the making of a trump, and I make it, can he play alone? *Answer.*—1. Your partner can play it alone. 2. You can play it alone. 3. You cannot. 4. Your opponent playing it alone bars you from so doing. 5. He cannot do so, having declined to take the responsibility of making the trump. The great fundamental rule of the game, in regard to playing alone, is this—only the parties can do so who take the responsibility of the trump, and are therefore liable to a euchre if they fail in their undertaking.

III. A, B, C, and D are playing Euchre. A and C are partners. A deals, B passes; C says: "I play it alone," and plays. A claims the right to play it alone after C says he plays it alone, and has played. The question is, has A a right to play alone after his partner says he plays it alone and plays? *Answer.*—A has no right to play it alone at all, after his partner, who had the first option, has elected to play alone. When C declared that he would play alone, it bound his opponents, and, by necessary consequence, equally bound himself and his partner. Therefore, the opponents have the right to keep A out of the game, and make C do that which he contracted to do—play alone.

IV. In four-handed Euchre, if the dealer throws his hand upon the table, having the two bowers, ace, king, and nine of trumps, can his left-hand adversary call for the nine of trumps upon his own lead of the queen? and must the dealer play the called card? in other words, in Euchre, as in Whist, does the showing of a card give an opponent the privilege of calling it? *Answer.*—In this special case the dealer would not be compelled to play the nine. The rule in Whist is in the nature of a penalty, and as there is no such special rule in Euchre, we must look at the *reason of the rule* to see whether it ought to apply to the case stated. Now in Whist, by exposing his card or cards a player gives knowledge to his partner; and hence the rule that such may be called for, and must be played. In the case submitted to us, the dealer, we assume, played alone. His hand was invincible. If one of his opponents had had all the other trumps, it would not have availed to stop the march. Hence, the dealer was not bound to play the nine on the queen. The stringent rule of Whist cannot be extended to Euchre in a case where the reason for the rule is wanting. It is a common practice for Euchre players who can infallibly take all the remaining tricks, to show, and they are conceded without the formality of separate play. The same principle applies to the case above. Under other circumstances, if a player shows a card, it can be called.

V. In a game of Euchre, A and B play against C and D. The trump is made by the latter. A and B having taken two tricks, C lays down his cards, which are both bowers and a king, and says he will bet he cannot be euchred. B, who sits at his left, and whose play it is, having ace and two trumps, takes the bet, claiming the right to call C's cards, he having exposed them, contending that, it being B's play, he had a right to play any card he pleased. Who was right? *Answer.*—C having laid down his cards, thereby exposing them, his opponents can call them as they think proper.

ALL-FOURS, AND PITCH.

I. At a game of All-fours, the parties are six each; one holds the jack and ace of trumps, and plays the former; it is taken by the queen, and the player claims the game, saying that the jack counts first. Who wins? *Answer.*—The jack does not count first, except when it is turned up, or when it is the highest card. It then counts as *high.*

II. In the course of play, A deals, and turns jack; B begs, and the cards are run; the same trump is turned, and they are run three further. In the last run there is a misdeal. Does A count for turning jack? *Answer.*—The jack counts; the misdeal did not take place until subsequent to its being turned. If the misdeal had been made previous to the jack being turned, or if there had been any doubt about it having been turned prior to the misdeal, the point could not have been scored. When a jack is turned, and a misdeal is made by reason of the pack being imperfect, the jack counts.

III. A, B, C, and D play a game of All-fours: spades were turned up. A led the ace of hearts, B played a heart, C trumped it, D played the four of clubs, and recalled it, saying: "I have a heart." He accordingly took back the club, and trumped the trick over C. A contended that he had no right to do it when he held the ten of hearts. Who is right? *Answer.*—D must play the ten of hearts in consequence of not having trumped over C on his first play. D cannot take advantage of his own wrong. *See No. V.*

IV. In playing a game of All-fours, A and C are partners against B and D. A having the deal, turns up a club for trump; B begs; A runs them and again turns up a club; he still continues, and once more turns up a club. The question is, can B insist that the dealer turn the last card for trump? *Answer.*—The last card must be turned, provided the cards have gone round equally. Should the *last card*, under these circumstances, be the same suit as the cards previously turned for trump, then the cards must be bunched, and dealt anew.

V. A and B are playing a game of All-fours. They are six each. A, in dealing, makes a misdeal, and turns a trump. B contends that he (A) has to deal over again, and claims that a man cannot lose his deal in All-fours. Who is right? *Answer.*—B is right. The dealer deals again, otherwise he might make a misdeal purposely for the sake of getting the beg. The reason is embodied in the law maxim, that "a man cannot take advantage of his own wrong." A forfeits the deal, if B chooses to claim it, for his misdeal. But when the misdeal is to A's manifest advantage, A has to deal again, otherwise he would "take advantage of his own wrong." This decision also applies to the game of Pitch.

VI. A, B, C, and D are playing All-fours. A deals, and turns up a spade. B begs, and A deals three more cards to each, and turns up the jack of spades. Does this jack—not being a trump, of course—count one point for A and partner? *Answer.*—It counts a point.

VII. A, B, and C are playing a game of Pitch. A deals, B pitches, and goes out on that hand. In the regular course, it would be B's deal and C's next pitch; but B being out of the game, must C deal, or can he claim his pitch? *Answer.*—C can claim his pitch, as it would be a manifest wrong to deprive him of that advantage, while at the same time A's rights would not thereby be in any way compromised or interfered with. The proper way, in a case of this kind, would be for B to deal C and A their hands, and then retire from the game.

The same point may arise in the game of All-fours, in relation to the beg, and is governed by the same rule.

VIII. A, B, and C are playing a game of All-fours. A is five, B two, and C is six; A deals and B begs. Has A the right to give one, thus putting C out, and continue the game between B and himself with the same hand? *Answer.*—He has. Supposing A to hold high and low in his hand, or either, it would be policy on his part to give one. And there is no restriction to the privilege of giving when an opponent begs.

IX. A game of All-fours is being played. The adversaries are six, and beg. The dealer, through inadvertence, gives, and of course puts his opponents out It is claimed that this cannot be done; that the game cannot be given away, but must be played to its conclusion; that the dealer has no power thus to relinquish it. *Answer.*—It *ought* not to be done, but it *can* be done. If the dealer gives when his adversaries are six, it is simply his fault. There is no rule of the game to prevent him from giving them, any more than there is when the others are five.

X. A party of four sat down to a game of All-fours. The dealer distributed six cards to each player and turned up the jack of clubs for trump. The eldest hand begged, and the dealer, not being able to give him one, run the cards, and clubs came trumps until the cards ran out. The dealer and his partner claimed a count for the jack, but their opponents in the game contended, that as the cards ran out, the jack could not be scored. Can a jack be counted when the cards run out? *Answer.*—The jack is counted.

CASSINO.

I. In playing a game of Cassino, A holds in his hand a deuce, ace, nine and ten. He plays his deuce on a seven lying on a table, making it nine; B, his opponent, cannot take it. Can A play his ace and make it ten? *Answer.*—He cannot, but if B had played an ace upon it, he (A) might have taken it with his ten. As it is, his best play is to take the nine he has "built up," with his nine in hand.

www.ingramcontent.com/pod-product-compliance
Lightning Source LLC
Chambersburg PA
CBHW030348170426
43202CB00010B/1299